STEPHEN TUROFF started his
but soon realized that he war..... ..
spiritual work. Now, with over forty years' experience, he is one of the best-known psychic therapists
in the world, working with the Power of Light to raise consciousness, bring inner balance and well-being. Stephen is also a teacher
of meditation and kriya yoga and holds seminars which lead to a
deeper understanding of who we are as human beings and the
purpose of our life in this world. Based in Essex, England, Stephen
continues to help numerous individuals with their personal development and healing, both in the UK and abroad. He is the author of
Seven Steps to Eternity.

LOVE, LOVE, LOVE
SPIRITUAL TEACHINGS

STEPHEN TUROFF

CLAIRVIEW

Clairview Books Ltd.,
Russet, Sandy Lane,
West Hoathly,
W. Sussex RH19 4QQ

www.clairviewbooks.com

Published by Clairview Books 2019

The right of Stephen Turoff to be identified as the author of this work has been asserted in accordance with sections 77 and 78 of the Copyright, Designs and Patents Act, 1988

A CIP catalogue record for this book is available from the British Library

Print book ISBN 978 1 912992 02 7
Ebook ISBN 978 1 912992 03 4

Cover by Morgan Creative
Typeset by DP Photosetting, Neath, West Glamorgan
Printed and bound by 4Edge Ltd, Essex

Contents

This book is made up of transcripts of seminars given by Stephen Turoff in Bled, Slovenia, between 2004 and 2008. Only minor edits and corrections have been made to the texts in order to retain the intimacy and immediacy of the original live events. Our thanks go to the Slovenian organizers of the seminars and to Emma Goldie for checking the manuscript.

1.

Love, Love, Love

God morning everybody. Maybe I'm in the graveyard? God morning everybody! I know you're very private people, but I didn't know you were *that* private that you can't even get into a graveyard! You think that's where you end up...? In the graveyard? Only the body — for you cannot die!

I wrote a little quote on here today: 'What is a true mark of a human being?' And it's so simple. Love, love, love. That's the simplicity of it. The mark of a true human being is love, love, love. Now, I decided — well I didn't decide — God decided, to call this seminar 'Love'. So we can't feel that love if we think we are a separate unit. We can only feel that love when we understand we are not separate. So the first thing we are going to do is for those of you that can, stand up. I want you just to turn to the person next to you, and hug them. Yes, yes, walk around, walk around.

You see, it's not a good morning, it's a God morning. See love, love, don't be afraid to love. Wonderful, you see, open your heart to it. You cannot put anything into a cup that is full of dirty water. Throw the old water out. Get ready to fill the cup with good stuff. How can God put love into your heart if it is so full of rubbish, so full of fear, so full of hate, so full of anger ... and violence? How can God put anything into a heart that is so full of this stuff? You have to pull it out first, pull this old stuff out. Don't allow yourself to live in fear. The moment you say 'yes' to God, God says 'yes' to you.

Even now some of you can't open your heart to God. Your mind is somewhere else. Don't you think God knows you? God knows you better than you know yourself. Why do we fill our hearts with this lie? We live a lie. Why is it so easy to lie instead of telling the truth?

You remember the words of Jesus. Speak the Truth and the Truth will set you free. He was talking to you and me. He was saying to you, live the Truth … you are wasting your life by not living the Truth. To live in the darkness when you can live in the light. To live in fear when you can live in love. What is this love that we're all looking for? Because if I was to ask any one of you, it would be a little different.

People live without love out of fear. Because when you are in love, you are in fear of losing it. You think you've never had it so good. And somebody will take that love away from me. But nobody can take true love away from you. First of all, you are born in love. I'm not just talking about biological parents. The divine father loves you. You see, this inner connection is what we need. Do you understand your potential? Not just as a human being, but as divinity! All the teachers who have ever come into the world tell us of this divinity that we have. Truly, you are made in the image of God, and of course, in our culture we have built up these images in statue, form, in words … we have called it God, Allah, Brahman. Many names we have given to this Force. But you see, who has called God, God? We have, we gave God the name God. We have no understanding of what this Force is, so we try to explain it in our language, in our feeling, and, with some people, with the expression. Some will say, well, 'God is love'; well, this is how we want to see and feel God. Some will say 'God is to be feared', because if you do not accept the law of God, he will punish you. What kind of God punishes you? All this has been built up in cultures. And from these cultures have come words, and from these words have come religions.

Religion gives us a way of life … or laws to live by. All cultures have been built upon religion. If you look even into your country and see how your country was built … It's written in now, into the constitution of your country. The same as every country in the world. Somewhere you will see the signs of religion. But true religion does not make you a prisoner. It does not put fear into you.

True religion sets you free, because you don't practice the religion, you practice spirituality. You practice the truth.

When you look at all the teachers in the world, all the spiritual teachers, they all give the same message. You are the Truth. You are born in the image of God. Why is it so hard to face the Truth? Why is it so hard to set yourself free from untruth? From our religion, our physical life as a human being, our country? There is always change ... Who makes the change? You do ... by how you think. You know, I always say, if the thinking is right, the action is right. Some would say thought, word and deed. Or, Father, Son and Holy Ghost.

To love unconditionally is only a word, because you don't know what unconditional love is. Why can't we express unconditional love? Because this world was not created for that. It was created as a play of duality. Of light and dark. Of love and hate. Of love and fear. Take your own lives. You know what it feels like to be in love. How quickly can that love be taken from you? It could be just one phone call. That's it. And your life can be upside down. Because this is our life of duality ... of attachments. We attach so much importance to things. We attach importance to things that are not permanent. We attach to the body ... the body is going to go. What can we really take to God with us? We can't take this body; we are going to say goodbye to it. And you have done this thousands of times. Not just once. You can't take your personality, your name or your fame. Or your wealth. You can be the richest person in the graveyard. What is that going to do for you? The only thing you can take with you is your truth. That's the only thing; you take your truth to God.

And you know, most people ... when you are standing there and God says: 'My child, what have you done?' You will lie. You won't mean to lie, but you will lie. You will say to God, 'God, I have done my best!' And you know you haven't done your best. You know it. Can you actually sit there now and tell me you have done your very best in your life? No you haven't. Oh you try ... We all try! But that's the difference between a Master ... and us. A Master doesn't change his mind. You see the Master knows ... God is too big to miss. You cannot miss God.

This brings the next question: 'Where is God?' And you have to answer the question with a question: 'Where is there no God?' You see, you think you are separate from God. In all religions they look up to heaven. But you see you are in heaven or hell now. Because it's a state of mind. What do you think is going to change when you die? Only the location. That's it. Location, location, location! It's the same when you buy a house, you know. Location, location, location. It's the truth.

You know the Masters do not change their mind. For them, there is only God. This is the hardest point for people to understand. That you are not separate from God. And God is not separate from you. There is no separation. What you have is amnesia. You have forgetfulness. You forget who you are. You forget where you have come from. You forget where you are going. This is the simplest question that all the Masters have to ask themselves: Who am I? Where have I come from? Where am I going? Three simple questions.

Let's write them down... Who am I? Where do I come from? Where am I going? Now, I know some of you will know the answer to this because the answer is very simple. But you see, just to know the answer isn't good enough. You have to put it into your heart. You see people say, 'God is in your heart'. Well of course, it's paradoxical because there is nowhere where God isn't. But to put the Force directly into the heart you have to take it from here [points to forehead] and bring it down into the heart chakra [draws hand down to heart]. This is what we have to do.

But let us look at this. Who am I? We are talking about the I. The answer is simple ... God. Where do I come from? God. Where am I going? God. Now, when you understand these words, it leads you on to the next aspect. And what does it say to you? If you put this together, what does it say to you? It says you have never left God. That there is nowhere to go. You have never gone anywhere. And you are not going anywhere, because truly, there is no place to go.

This was why God was created. God is the word we gave the energy, the process. Life is God, God is life. Life is a process. Whatever you do against life, life has a way of changing, to safeguard itself . . . to evolve. That's how life was created. You see, God is not separate from life. People have this impression that this is all life and God is up here [stands on chair], looking down. Again, it's paradoxical, because yes, God is looking up and God is looking down. When you understand there is only God, you will understand that there is only one of us here. There is only one soul, not many souls. That's the great illusion. That's the great lie. There was no one to know who I was, so I created all that is . . .

Now it gets complicated. Should love be complicated? No! Love for the sake of loving. When you love from the soul, you love from that highest point of realization. When you love from the human mind, you are in dangerous waters. Because it always changes. What the mind wants today, the mind doesn't want tomorrow. Always in a state of flux. But when the soul loves, the soul loves from the point of view of just loving. And when it looks at you, it sees itself. But when the mind looks at another person, it only sees the personality. This is what the Masters do, see? You see the Masters, they are very clever. They don't just love God. They see God in everything. Do you know, when we were children we had a game in England we called hide and seek? Well it's the same with God. God is hiding everywhere.

Look at the tree; when I look at a tree, I say, God I see you . . . you can't hide from me. When I look at a flower, God I see you! You can't hide from me. When I breathe the air, God I feel you! You cannot hide from me. When I look at an animal, God I see you! You cannot hide from me. When I look at you . . . God I see you! You cannot hide from me! Because I love you unconditionally, I cannot live in fear of you. I step out of that game, of love and fear. In other words; I balance myself. People say to me: 'Stephen, you know, you are so down to earth, but you get all these lights appear, God speaking and all this stuff happening.' It's because I have my feet on the ground, but my mind, my head, is in God, to balance everything.

You see, if you listen to the words of the Masters: What did Jesus say to us? Turn the other cheek. Try to understand the philosophy behind what he said. If we attach to the action, there is a reaction. Watch ... [pushes colleague suddenly but gently; she jumps and gasps ... then hugs and reassures her]. There's an action and a reaction. All the time. And this is how human beings are: we act and we watch, we act and we watch. And this is what makes us live in such a world as today. Because you know, in our hearts we always want to act right. But sometimes the head gets in the way. And instead of expressing love, we express fear. The head takes over. From our fear comes our anger, and from our anger comes violence. From one to the other, from countryman to countryman. From country to country.

What are we doing? Why are we doing it? Is it an inbuilt thing? Is it a part of the process? Well of course it is! Because from that process we evolve. You know, if you take 2,000 years ago to today, we've evolved scientifically, and we are evolving spiritually. But the way we are evolving, we are forgetting who we are. I told you, God is everything. He is the very nature of everything, the nature of life itself. Look how we are abusing it, and every one of us here is guilty of it. And you know, we turn our backs on it, because we say: 'What can I do?' Well, generally the war only starts with one person.

Of course, you can change. Don't try to change the world. Change yourself. Give love a chance. Give this soul, that is your very essence, a chance. If I was to say to you: 'How do you want to live?' You will say: 'In peace.' But look at you – you are not in peace; most of you are in pieces! Oh, you put on this little smile. You put this on [reaches for glasses]: I can't see without my glasses on. Where are my eyes? We don't live in peace, we live in pieces. Oh, but I want to be happy! Explain to me what happiness is? What is happiness? 'Being in peace with yourself.' Being in peace with yourself. Inner peace. Everybody has his own image in his head. Some people would take a big chopper and chop you up and be happy doing it! You see, happiness means something different to everybody.

For me, happiness is a moment between two evils, because today you could be very happy, and tomorrow you could have a gun in your hand. Or even in the next moment it could change like that . . . Why does it happen? It happens because you can't love yourself, so you want to love something or somebody else, hoping that they will love you back; hoping that they will need you. And if you don't get it in the way you want it, God help us! Because then the old fear comes out, and the anger comes out, and the violence comes out. Do you know it's harder to live like that than it is to live with love and peace? Wouldn't you like to live without fear? Do you always want to live in fear? Do you always want to live in anger? Do you want to go against your very nature?

The true nature of a human being is to love. We've evolved from the caveman. We don't have to take our club anymore and hit somebody on the head. The club we use now is our expression. When you say 'I love you' to somebody, say it from the heart . . . not just from the mind. Try next time; remember the hide and seek. God is there in front of you. See God within that person. Okay, you may not like their personality, that's understandable. People say to me: 'But Stephen, you love everybody?' Yes I do. But I may not love their actions. I can do little about their actions, but do I love them? Of course. Otherwise my whole philosophy falls to pieces. I love God. That means I have to love myself. And while I am in this duality, I have to love the aspects of God. And each one of you is an aspect: a divine aspect. I love you, that's it. There's no 'whys' or 'wheres' or 'hows' or 'what'. I don't care if you're black, white, pink or blue. I'm not concerned if you are Muslim, Hindu, Jew or Christian. I'm concerned only with you as a human being; that while you are in this game of life, let's evolve together. Let us all join together. This is what joining is about.

Do you think you are separate from God? So, now is the time for rejoining! All the world, all the population of the world, is a part of you. You are not separate from any of it. The power, the love is made manifest . . . all around you. You have to be blind not to see it. Jesus said that you have eyes but you are blind. You have ears but you are deaf. Listen and you can hear the voice of God speaking to you. He has so many ways of speaking to you: through nature, the wind, stars, trees, the birds, through us.

I want to tell you a story. I have told you this story before but I will tell you this story again. I was in a waiting room and I said to God, 'God, I love you very much'. And instantly there was a reaction from God. About seven foot away from me, up by the ceiling, came a very loud voice . . . VERY LOUD! This voice came out of the air, and the voice said: 'My beloved son, I love you.' That's it. The voice was as clear as I am speaking to you now. Most of you know that when these manifestations happen around me, there are always witnesses. But there was no witness this time. This was for me. You see, God will speak with us. People say: 'Well, why doesn't God open the door to me?' Well you see, you have to be a little bit clever, you have to knock on the door louder than anybody else. And you have to keep knocking on it until God opens it. Then you will see a difference in your life.

Yoga and mysticism are words, an expression, but true yoga is living it. To live it. You know, when light hits darkness, a war always goes on. Now, why have I said that? Because there's many pictures that are taken of me where I extend light. In the last seminar we did, there was light coming out of my head, and we have that on film. And also, if some of you were there, you'd have heard sounds in the air. Like music appearing in the air. There's many . . . you know, I always get so excited talking about experiences with God. And do you think I make mistakes? Yes I do.

I can remember when these lights first started to appear, and people were filming them. I said to God: 'God I don't need this, why are you giving me this?' And God said: 'So you think they are for you?' How simple to make a mistake, huh? To let your ego get in.

You don't realize. Then I realized that what was happening around me was for people. To share it with people. And it was quite strange when it first started to happen. I can even remember being in Israel, and the national newspaper came to do an article. And as they filmed me, I dematerialized in front of them, and they filmed it happening. And the headlines in their paper read: 'Magician'! Not how did I do it, not what is happening – just, 'magician'. But in truth, we are all magicians. All of us have the ability within us to do these wonderful things.

Didn't Jesus say: 'greater things than this shall ye do'? Didn't he say that? Who was he talking to? He was talking to you, me, to the Masters. A Master doesn't wake up one day and say, 'Oh I'm going to be a Master.' A saint doesn't wake up and say, 'Oh I'm going to be a saint!' You know, you have to be dead to be a saint, yeah? You know how it works don't you? You know, first of all people call you a Master ... then they look upon you and treat you with wonder ... then all of a sudden they get angry ... from their anger they crucify you ... after they crucify you ... they call you a saint! Wonderful way of life, isn't it? So if your ambition is to be a saint ... we can help you there. Don't try to be a saint, just try to be a human being. But a good human being. That's it.

Now a lot of people come to Masters because they want to hear something very special. They want a short cut to God. The Master has hidden knowledge. Well? The knowledge is not hidden. It's inside of you. Go within. This is what a Master has done. You see, a Master starts off like you. They have an ambition or a desire. Their desire is God. That's what they want. So they start searching ... like you and like me. They get into something called yoga, meditation and mystical knowledge. They take time out to study that knowledge, and to put that knowledge into practice. They don't turn around and say: 'Oh, I don't have time to meditate!' They make time. Some of these Masters were working people like you and me. They would work all day, but at night, they would spend the night in meditation, connecting with the inner self. Learning about the inner self. How to bring that Divine energy into the physical world. Of course, it's an art and it's a science.

This is what yoga is, it's a science. It's a science of union. This is what yoga means, union. Union with the self. Of course, we have to conquer different aspects of the lower self to allow the higher self to be manifest. You will see this sign in life: the triangle. Now, what does it represent? Well the first thing that hits you is the [all seeing] eye. What is this eye? Well, it's symbolic of the 'I am'. The eye is watching you; it's watching everything. In other words, it is the Absolute. I AM. Because it is watching everything. I said to you, God is an energy. God is the process of life itself. You – if you want to use the word God or life – is what you are. But who put that into process? We gave this energy a name; we called it God. But this energy is what you are. You are not separate from it.

What does that make you? It makes you the Creator. And of course, sitting here you don't feel much like the Creator do you? But let's just look at this. Look at these two beautiful people that have been singing to us. Weren't they creating music? They were creating sound. There you see God creating. You see, when you think of Creation of God, you look like this. You only see the big things. And if you say, yes I am God, you say: 'How can I make the earth?' But, oh, you can! The same as you can make sound. If you can destroy the earth, which man is doing now, you can recreate it. The same as yourselves. You are recreating yourself, every single day. Every moment, you are recreating yourself. You are creating yourself into the person you want to be. Some would say out of choice, some would say not out of choice. But you always have a choice. It's a choice of being empowered or a choice of being disempowered. It's up to you … you're creating your reality now. Right this very moment.

Now, the hard part to understand is that you are not only creating this reality – and you are playing the role of the lover, or of the person who lives in fear – you are also watching it take place. You see, because God is all there is, here there is no wrong or right, there just *is*. To take what best serves you, to take what best serves your society — that makes your society flourish — with and in contrast with God's law... And one of these laws is cause and effect; as you sow, so you reap, or the law of karma. I tell you, truly, love sets you free. Love does not make you a prisoner. When you are in love, you can walk on the clouds; when you are in love you can walk on water; when you are in love you can turn that water to wine. This is what love does for you. It gives you freedom — freedom to express yourself as you want yourself to be. Not to be what somebody else wants you to be. Not to live in somebody else's shadow, but to live without fear, without fear of anybody or anything.

People have fear of dying. I'd say no, you don't have fear of dying, you have fear of living, because death is going to come upon all of us. It's like a shadow that follows us around, ready to strike at any time. Be ready for it. What should be our readiness? In the name of God. The name of God should be on our lips. The name of God should be pounding in our hearts. Make no mistake. God is the true reality. If you cannot believe in that now, there will come a time when you will believe in it. And then you will go beyond belief. You will go into a knowing; and then the knowing will change, into the known.

People say to me: 'Stephen do you believe in God?' My immediate reaction is: 'No.' I don't need to believe in God. I know God exists. There's no belief — no belief from my part at all. How do we know God is love? We don't, we presume God is love. Because, this is what we want to feel. It's the same as some of the cultures that believe God is hate. They live it, and they murder and kill in that name. So you see, there's always a duality taking place: light and dark, light and dark. But all the time, the all-seeing eye is ever upon us [draws picture of eye within a triangle]. So, all the time, you could say, God is watching us.

Now, why the triangle? Put into your mind: Father, Son and Holy Ghost. Put this into your mind. I am giving you wisdom here that you won't find in a book. Now, the bottom of the triangle — we can say the base of life – is based on wisdom. Knowing how to do things, that is knowledge, but wisdom comes with experience; knowledge without wisdom is dangerous. It can create many wars. Now, when we look to the left of the triangle, we see growth. What makes a child grow? When you hold the child in your arms! What makes the child grow? Okay, you're going to say food, but no … love. Love. Love, you see – love makes the child grow. So love, wisdom, love. But you see, it takes something else. There is something else that has to be added, because you know love is wonderful. But you see, to have love there has to be action. And if there's action, there has to be reaction. So, there's an energy. What is the energy? It's power … So Wisdom, Love and Power.

Now, when these are in perfect harmony, it creates another energy. In other words, it centralizes, it centralizes you as a human being. When all these three energies are in perfect balance, they create peace. It's when these energies are not in balance that you are in pieces. Peace is within … inside of you. The same as anger is inside of you. This is the choice you have. When these energies are out of balance, there is fear. Simple as that.

Where is the love? What are you doing with your life? These are the questions you start to ask yourself. You ask: 'Do I want this anymore?' Most of you don't. You know, if you look at your life – if there's something in your life that you want to change … Maybe there's something in your work you want to change? There's always something we want to change because we're not happy with it. There's only one thing you have to ask yourself. Does it best serve you? What you are living now – does it best serve you as a human being? If the answer is yes, then continue … if the answer is no, then change it. You can change anything in your life if you want to. But once all these energies are in perfect balance, Love is the outcome, or Harmony, or Bliss.

Let's look at this word bliss, because we hear a lot about it. Why be happy when you can change that happiness? Why shouldn't we have something that is more permanent? Okay, so between fear and love if we have a perfect balance; but because you are living in duality, you cannot get rid of fear or love, but you can balance it. Within this balance, there is a state of being. The state of being is called Bliss... Perfect Harmony. How do we get like that? By being yourself. Now remember, being *the self*. There is a difference: of being yourself, and being the self. Because being yourself, half of you doesn't love yourself, so that's a negative, isn't it? That's fear. But being the self is a positive. And you're thinking: 'God, that is so hard to do that.' It's not. I would say it's harder being like you are, than being the self. Yes? You know what I mean, don't you? Because sometimes being this self here is false. It's a lie, because you are being what you don't want to be. Or, you are trying to be what somebody else wants you to be.

Look, when you first ... I don't know if it's your wife or your lover or girlfriend ... All I know is that when you first meet, you fall in love with that person. You fall in love with all of them. The little things they do. Their looks, their laughter, their jokes, their strengths, their weaknesses. You fall in love with the whole of the person. And you accept them for what they are – that's what you fall in love with. So why do we try to change it? After one or two or three years of being together. Why do we try to change it? You try to change it into what you want. In other words, you try to disempower your partner. And you know a partner can only be disempowered if you let them. That's not love. That's demonic. Now, why does that happen? It happens out of fear. It happens because you are not in balance.

These energies of wisdom that you all have... You have the knowledge, but you are not using your wisdom. Wisdom comes with experience. Now knowledge without wisdom, I told you, is dangerous, because it puts you in fear. If there is no wisdom, how can you understand the true power of love, when you are in dis-harmony? And then what happens? The body becomes dis-at-ease. So disease manifests itself. Of course, it's a lot deeper than I have explained it to you. But let's just touch the surface first. Maybe at some stage I will run much deeper mystical seminars, because I don't want to frighten you off completely. Because I can give you exercises to do, that will enhance your powers. What perfume do you like? 'Gucci?' I don't know what Gucci … I don't know … [makes a motion with his hand]. Gucci, yeah Gucci. [A smell of Gucci perfume appears.]

Love, love, love. You see, just love. Love sets you free from all this. That's what every teacher has tried to give you. You are truly born in love. The truth of that is, of course, God. Wow … Sandalwood. It's just appearing! Of course all this, I tell you again, is based on love, love, love. There's nothing else for you to do. You just have to open your eyes … and see it. You know it's … You're so close to it. You cannot believe you can walk into it like this, and you can walk out of it like this.

Separating us from full realization of God, there's only a dividing line. That's all it is. But you see, most people are in fear of crossing the line. And you know why? Because they think they are going to lose their power. But it's the opposite. Your power increases. But it's a different kind of power: the power that says 'Yes'. Not this negative power that says 'No'. Look, I have been at both ends. Every Master has had their dark periods. I told you, a Master doesn't wake up and say, 'Oh I'm a Master today!' They have their dark periods. But they come out of them. They see them for what they are. They become building blocks of our character. They are ghosts of the past and of the present, but not of the future. You see – today … No, no, let's put it another way …

Every time you go to sleep at night, you die. You die. You don't know anything. You don't know if you are going to wake up. You don't know what is happening. Things have shut down. And you go to sleep. And you wake up in the morning – 'hopefully', you wake up in the morning [laughs] and it is a new 'birth-day'. It's a new birth-day. Now, when it is your birthday, people give you gifts. They give you a card and they may give you a present, and they say, 'Happy Birthday!' They say: 'How old are you?' 'Oh, oh I'm 21!' [laughs]. For the last 50 years I've been 21 [laughs].

But it's the same with God. See, you wake up. It's a new birth-day. And God gives you a gift. What is the gift? We call it the present. God gives us a present – in other words he gives us *the present*. Not the past, not the future, but *the present*. The very present. Because past, present and future are one. It's all happening now. But your conscious reality is in the present. And for those that have conscious understanding of divinity, they don't live in the present, they live in *the presence*. I call this stage, the stage of 'Is'. 'Is-ness.' Some of you will know it as 'being-ness'.

About two years ago, I reached this stage. And … very many things happen when you reach this stage. One of the things is that you can 'time-shift'. And they were filming me time-shift, and there were many photos where you can see me time-shift. But also the whole room would time-shift. This is because the past, the present, the future, is one. I am all there is. Now, how do you get to this stage? Now, this is going to be paradoxical: by not wanting to get to that stage; by becoming *desire-less*. This is where the paradox is – because there is a desire to be; and the moment you have desire, you create an action and you create a reaction. So the reaction is *magnetism* – so desire creates magnetism. And when you create magnetism, it can either draw you to me, or push you away from me.

Stand up here. I don't know if I can do this but I will try. You see, magnetism is what your life is based on, because it draws and it pushes. You see, it's the law of cause and effect. The law of attraction and the law of repulsion. You know, it's like when you see … I can only speak from a man's point of view – I can't speak from a woman's point of view. Like – when you're younger of course, not my age now, when you're younger – when you see a beautiful woman, you go: 'Wow!!!' [Stalks around like a cockerel – audience laughter.] At my age it's 'Oh … okay …'. But you see, okay, there's an attraction. There's a hormone thing going on. And you know it must be the same for a woman. That's because God made us equal. [Audience agrees.] Okay! So, you see the man sees the woman …

'Wooow...' The woman sees the man and... 'Wooow' – and you know they want to come together. This is the law of attraction. You do your thing, then maybe the woman says: 'Oh I've got a headache' [audience laughter], then, 'oh, not today'. You see the law of repulsion. The law of attraction is saying: 'I want to join, I don't want to be separate anymore. I want to join back.' But you see, the individuality is saying: 'Oh no, I like being me, I like to be separate, I'm a man.'

I don't know, I think it's stronger to be a woman than a man. Believe me, I thank God every day that God never made me a woman in this life. I don't know about the weaker sex; believe me, I think the women are the stronger sex. I could not have a baby – no thank you. But of course, I have had to experience it in another lifetime. Next one: no, I wanna be a man again in the next one! Who knows, it's up to Him. He's already told me where my next life is anyway... Where? Africa. What is the difference if I am in England or... My last life – I was in India. But God decided to put me in England. You know, you most fear ... maybe you fear the black man, maybe you fear the yellow man, the red man, the white man? But maybe you were the red man in your last life? Maybe you were the black man, the white man, the yellow man? You see, we have to experience everything.

How do you know what is hot, if you don't know what is cold? How can you experience love, until you experience fear? You see, it's the opposite side of the same coin. This is your duality. In other words, the Masters say: 'This is a game'. Well, you know all games have rules. Just learn the rules to the game and it becomes fun. Don't get tired playing the game. Learn the rules ... and you will not sit there looking like this ... [slumps and pulls a grumpy face]. You will be going [smiles triumphantly]: 'Wow, isn't this a great game?'

You have so little time in this physical life. Why waste it with fear and hate, when you can live it as you really, truly want to live it? From the soul level. Not from the mind level. Because you know, the soul is free. Before you came here, you were the Master. You were ecstatically in love. But you decided to experience the opposite of what you were. The only way you could do that is to go into the darkness, so you took a body. And you know, when you take a body on, you take on two slaves. The first slave is the body, the second slave is the mind. And the soul is the Master. But my God, look at you! You don't look like Masters to me . . . Why is that? Now you are no longer the Master. The mind is the Master, and you are the slave. And you run behind the body. Like a dog. And the mind, you know, is very clever, it gets food from the table, and throws it to the dog. Scraps of food from the table. If you were standing there and somebody got food from the table and threw it to you, would you eat it? Maybe if you were starving. But you would rebel; you wouldn't accept that way of life. But why do you accept the scraps off the table when you can have the whole feast . . . Why? What have you done? You have given your power over to the mind. In other words, you have disempowered yourself. And you have empowered your mind to take control. It's time to take back your power . . . to say, 'Yes'. To re-empower yourself. To Stand Up, and say *Yes* to the self, and *No* to the mind. Finish the mind games. They will destroy you. They will hunt you to the grave . . . and beyond the grave. Because you cannot escape them.

Even when you pass from this life, it follows you [points to head]. You still have a mind, you have a body; it will answer to your name. If you think you are going to die and have a pair of wings, playing a harp, forget it. If you think you are going to die and you're going to have a pair of these [makes horns on his head with fingers], forget it! Heaven and hell don't exist. But what does exist are your thoughts, and they can be a living hell. I don't have to tell this to you — you know this. Some of you have already experienced this. And it's not nice; it's not nice at all.

We need medication. We need to take vitamins. And the vitamin we need to take is Vitamin G. Take it, it's free. You can get very high on it. It makes you strong. And that is Vitamin God. Fill your body with it. Fill your mind with it. Take back your power. Say Yes to the self. Too long you have been saying No, no, no ... and look at what has happened to you. Time to say, Yes. Yes God ... Do you know, it is such a powerful mantra. People say to me: 'Tell me a mantra that is magic.' Yes I can give you mantras; I can give you a mantra that will materialize Shiva energy. I've used it several times here. But this is not magic. It's knowledge with wisdom.

How many of you today said, 'Thank you, God' [a few hands rise in the audience]. You see, only a few of you. But it should be said all the time. You see, this is such a small mantra. But the *power* behind it, and the *power it brings*, is tremendous. Because God said to us: even before you ask, I have given it to you. So we say 'thank you' before we receive it. Well of course, we *would* say thank you, but if you are very in pain, you won't say 'thank you, God'. I remember falling down in great pain once, and before I passed out, I said 'thank you, God — it doesn't matter how much pain you give me. If you think that will change my mind about you, You are mistaken!'

I don't love easily, but when I love, I love with passion. Love with *passion*. I love God with the passion of a thousand suns. Look in the eyes of anybody that's in love. Look at their eyes. That tells you if they are in love or not, because their eyes will burn with the passion of a thousand stars. It doesn't matter what words come out of your lips, how you want to act — the eyes are the windows of the soul that cannot lie. Sometimes the windows are dirty, so we have to get busy to clean them. To let the sun shine — our spirituality — shine through. It's the same with this ... [walks to the window]. You see, the mind is dark [draws curtain]. But when you draw the curtain, the light comes in. You see, it's the same here [points to head]. Clean the windows of the mind of the soul. Get busy, don't leave it. You will see the magic of it. You will see your fear run away from the light. It will give a whole new meaning to your life. You won't feel separate anymore. It's because you feel separate that you live with your fear. You don't feel in unity, you live in disunity. So a war goes on in the mind. Take back your power. Say 'yes' to yourself!

The other mantra I use, is Yes, God ... Yes, God ... Yes, God ...

Yes, God ... Yes, God ... Yes, God ... Yes, God ... Smell ... Can you smell it? Can you smell it? [Whispers.] Yes, God ... Yes, God. You see, you are speaking with God and God is speaking with you. And you are answering God; you are saying, 'Yes, God.' Because at this higher level, you are in communication with the higher self all the time.

There are two hemispheres to the mind. There is the hemisphere of the higher mind [draws triangle with 'all-seeing eye'] and the lower mind. But there is a filter. There is a filter, you see, in the higher mind where there is light, to where there is dark in the lower mind. My spelling isn't very good today. I do well – you see, I am dyslexic. I do very well! So you see the light of the all-seeing eye, from the soul level to the body. You have the downward triangle, or man into matter, and then up man into light.

So, what you are aiming for is to realize the light; some would say, to get back to it. But in truth, there is no back. You are it. There's nowhere to go. Nowhere to go. Except to be. And all it is, is this dividing line. Because let us say, from there it gets heavier. Now, not just mentally does it get heavier, but the whole of evolution. This would be man into matter – and God was so clever that he had to do something. God cannot help being God. God is God. Everything you see, everything you don't see, everything you hear, everything you don't hear, is God. So why do you think you are separate? What has created this separateness? Here, the mind. The mind, that is the cleverness of God. That's how clever you are. So, you had to create a plan. The plan was to forget who you are, but with the added knowledge that you can get out of this at any time – when you've had enough of the game, when you want to have a rest. You may want to rest for a thousand years, because what is time? Remember what I said: past, present and future is one. Time is expressed through motion, through distance. The nearest your scientists have got to God so far is quantum physics. It is very close to saying: 'Yes, an intelligence rules the universe.' And that's something for scientists to admit. Yes, God exists, because I exist; and all that exists is I.

So, are you happy with living in the darkness? Are you happy living in the lower mind? And if not, change it! As a matter of fact, you can move in and out of this. You see I'm playing safe. I have one foot in the box and one foot out of the box. I love the game – when I want to play the game, I jump inside the box. When I want to come out of it, I just step out of it. But I never forget, *Who Am I?* This is why I started off today with speaking the Truth. This is what Jesus said, speak the Truth and the Truth will set you free. The first person you have to speak the Truth to is yourself. Don't try to tell other people the Truth when you don't know it yourself. How can you?

You know, people say to me: 'What should I look for in a teacher?' Because you see all these teachers advertising, these Masters advertising. And they want to follow a Guru, a Teacher. There's only one thing you have to ask a teacher or Master: Have you had any direct experience of God? Direct experience. That's all you have to ask yourself. You see, in truth, what could be hurt? I cannot be hurt, but the ego can be hurt. The higher mind, which is the I, can't be hurt; it is unchanging, undamaging, but the lower mind, oh, it can suffer. You see, we have *the ego*. It's the ego that gets hurt; *you* can't be hurt – how can a Master be hurt? If you are a Master, you have mastered the I. If you are not a Master, you are only trying to master the ego. And it is this that will give you pain.

Now, what should we do? Put a line between the ego: 'e' and 'go': 'e-go'. Let it go, don't suffer it. It doesn't matter what people want to think of you. If you go out of here loving me, if you go out of here hating me . . . I love you. Why should what you think of me change it? I get tired of these games, and the pains... You can't see? Can everybody see this? Maybe you should have binoculars. But you're welcome to come up of course, after, and look and maybe ask me any questions. You see, when I am talking about the windows of the mind, there's many windows. But what is a window? Something that we see through. It lets in light. That's it. You look through it – all the time you are looking through this. Why do you think in your meditation that you end up seeing light? Because this is what you are.

What does the Bible tell us? You are made in the image of God. What is the image of God? How do you perceive God? You know, people perceive God as light. Now, let's get to the next thing, because this is wonderful... Scientists say to us: 'Ahh, we are made up of matter, of electrons, neutrons, protons, photons, *lifetrons* – and lifetrons are the finest vibration of matter. And okay, so, of course, they enquire: How is matter made up? Well, they say: 'Oh, matter is condensed energy, so squeezed together that the energy becomes solid, or it looks solid.' Because look, you touch yourself, it's solid to you. You touch this [presses against wall], it's solid. But you know, nothing is solid. Everything vibrates, everything is in a state of movement. So energy is condensed into matter.

So of course, the next question is: How is energy created? Now they are coming up with light. Light is condensed into energy, energy is condensed into matter. This is why we say, or Jesus says, speak the Truth, because when you speak the Truth, you speak with a power of the Father, of the Son and of the Holy Ghost. When this is united, the Father is wisdom, the Son is love, and the power is the Holy Ghost. And when you are balanced with this, you speak with the Truth of God. In other words, you speak with the Light of God. You speak in the Absolute Truth.

Now, when I was in Spain giving a talk on love like this, the light was coming out of my mouth ... and they filmed it happening. You can get one of these pictures at the back ... You see the light coming out of my mouth? It's not clever, it's not a trick. It's about the Self. It's about being one with the Truth. See, people say God is the Truth ... That is not the Truth. The Truth is God. That's the Truth. That's how subtle it is. But don't try to tell the Truth to the world. Start with yourself. Tell the truth to yourself. Start small. Bring your truth into your reality. The Truth comes from the higher Self, it's that highest feeling. That feeling that says 'Yes, God'. Not 'No, God'.

So, the I lives in the Light. It lives in the Light because it is the

Light. It is the Wisdom. It is the Love. It is the Power. You cannot take any of that away from God. Even if you deny God – even if you hate God! If you don't love God, God loves you. Because he loves unconditionally. He puts no condition on it. He loves you for you. Even with the things we have done in our lives, and none of us have been saints. Well, maybe not in this lifetime, anyway. I was saying to someone: 'One of the biggest saints of India started off being a highway robber, and he would kill people.' Yes. Would you like to hear the story?

There was a robber who used to live near the woods, and he killed many people and robbed them. He became a very famous robber. One day, three monks were walking through the woods, and this robber jumped out with a sword and he said: 'Give me your money.' And the monk said 'My son, we have no money.' And the robber says: 'Well, if you have no money I will have to kill you.' And the monk said: 'But why do you have to kill me?' And the robber said: 'Well, people will think I am weak if I don't kill you, and they won't fear me!' And the monk said: 'My son, do you realize the bad karma that you are creating for yourself? Does your family agree with you doing this?' And the robber said: 'Of course they agree.' So the monk said: 'Look, before you kill us, just do one thing. Go home to your wife, ask her, ask your family – will they share your bad karma?' So the robber said: 'Hah, so you think I am stupid? I will go home and you will run away!' And the monk says: 'No, no, no, no. I give you our word. We'll stay here. And if you take our body . . . if you want to kill us, kill us. But we will be here when you come back.' 'Well, okay!' So, he goes home.

And his family, two children and his wife, were there. And he says: 'I've had a very strange experience.' And he relates the story to his wife. And he says to his wife: 'Will you share my karma?' She says 'Of course not! It is your *dharma*, your duty to feed us!' And the children say: 'No, we will not share your karma!' You see, he was so shocked, because before he thought he was doing the right thing for his family. There was a change in his mind. He just stepped up a little bit, to self-consciousness. In other words, he came out of the darkness.

So, he went back to the three monks. And the monks were still standing there. And one monk said: 'Well, my son?' And the man said: 'You are right. You are so right. What can I do? I want to follow you. I am very sad about what I have been doing.' So they said: 'If you want to follow us, you have to say the name of God – keep chanting the name of God.' But he was so evil that he couldn't even say the name of Rama or God. So they said to him: 'Okay, you can follow but you can say Ra. Just say Ra!' So he could say 'Ra'!

So, the months and years went by, and he followed the monks everywhere. But slowly, the words coming from his lips changed: 'Ra ... Ra ... Ra ... Ra ... Ra ... Ra ... Ra ... Ram ... Ram ... Ram ... Ram ... Ram ... Ram ... Ram ... Rama ... Rama ... Rama ... Rama ... Rama ...' So he started here – in the lower mind – and he ended up here – the I, higher mind – with all the evil he did. And he wrote the epic *Ramayana*, and it was Swami Valmiki. Swami Valmiki. Yes. And his name became Swami Valmiki, very famous saint of India. And this is not just one case that has happened. What does it tell you? It tells you that as low as you sink, as high you can climb. When you have tasted the honey ... you won't want to eat anything else. Honey is God. Why do you think the yogis sit there with a big smile on their face? Because their stomach is full of honey. Yes, and when you know you are in love with God, and you're having his honey, you taste it on your lips.

Let me give you an example of this. A few years ago, maybe three years ago, I can't remember now, I was working in the surgery. There were about 32 people in the waiting room. And I was in one of the surgery rooms. And I couldn't work – the energy was too strong. So I went into the waiting room and I said: 'Look, can you all please go outside, the energy is too strong. Something is wrong.' When we went outside, Shiva was above the surgery, and the people saw this. So I came to get some water. All the water turned to rose water, and as I was standing there, honey was running from my hands. So I went outside where the people were standing to give the water and honey to people, and they were filming me. And as they filmed me a *Shiva Lingam*[*] came from my stomach.

God is honey, Amrita, and when you taste the sweetness of it: Wow! You are hooked like a fish on a line. God just reels you in, like a fisherman; God reels you in. I tell you, my brothers and sisters, when you taste the honey of God, nothing else will do — literally, I mean that. You may have the lovely houses, the lovely cars, the lovely suits, everything. And my advice is to enjoy everything God gives you. Don't be afraid to spend what energy you have. Only living in fear creates the situation where you are afraid.

Because money is an energy, use it, play the game; if you give, you'll receive — you give, you receive, that's the law. What goes out must come back. The more you give, the more you receive. That's how it works, I know. If I have a desire for something, somehow God gives it to me. Thank you very much! And I enjoy the gifts of God. I remember many years ago I bought a car, and I took two friends out in the car, and that night (they were a married couple) — that night a *Baba* appeared physically to the couple and said to them, 'What do you think of my new car?' And I've had many experiences like this. Wonderful, because it is God's car. That's the truth. I am God, but so are you. That's it, that's the Truth; Remember, live the Truth and the Truth sets you free. Live it, don't deny the Truth to yourself because some book wants to put you into sin.

Let's look at this sin. If you're not married and you have a child — sinful. And when a child — you know we've all been children, haven't we? And what does a child do? It doesn't like clothes on; and you know, a child explores itself — it's natural. But if the parents see it, they say: 'This is sinful, you must not do this.' And all of a sudden, fear is created. Where does that fear go? It goes inside. And you know, the child grows up. It goes to work — that is not sinful if you

---

[*] A representation of the Hindu deity Shiva.

go to work. But it is sinful if you earn too much money! True? It's true. It's sinful if you work too much. I have a habit of working too much. It's wonderful to get married. It's not sinful to get married. It's not sinful to go to church, but it's sinful to go to the wrong church. Wow, have you ever experienced that?

I want to tell you a story, and this is a very true story. I had a phone call, and the man said to me: 'I am phoning in relation to my brother. My brother has got only two weeks to live. He has cancer, he has two weeks to live and he's in a hospice. Can we bring him to see you?' I said, 'Yes.' He said, 'But there's only one problem. He's a Roman Catholic bishop.' I said, 'No problem, bring him!' So I met him, and he told me, 'They've given me two weeks to live.' The doctors opened him up, and he was full of cancer, and they sewed him up. He said, 'They've given me two weeks, but two weeks is not long enough to get my house in order. I need eighteen months!' So I said, 'Okay, I've asked God.' And God said, 'Yes.' So I said: 'God has given you eighteen months.' He was so happy, they went away.

A week later I got a phone call. All the cancer had gone, and he was completely cured. He was so happy that he wanted to come and work with me. And he did. And one of the patients that come to see us, he was ... sorry, I'm being taken over, sorry ... he was possessed. So this young man came and laid on the bed. The bishop had this big cross and stood there with his hands on the young man's feet. The cross was laying over like this. I was at the head of the young man, performing the exorcism. All of a sudden, there was a wind in the room, and the cross of the bishop was spinning around like this ... like crazy! Anyway, we managed to help the young man, and help the soul that was controlling this young man.

The very next day I got a phone call from the bishop. He started to shout down the phone: 'I'm a marked man, I've been marked, I've been marked.' I said, 'Explain.' He said: 'I've got the crucifixion marks come up in my hands, in the side, in the feet.' And he came to show me. No blood but big marks, right the way through his hands, his feet and in his side. And on the eighteenth month ... he was gone! Beautiful!

I want to tell you one more story. Now that was a Roman Catholic bishop. This other story is about a Church of England vicar. I got a phone call: 'We have a man who is in a wheelchair, he has a brain tumour, he can't walk. Can we bring him to see you?' I said, 'Certainly!' So they brought him in. There was the man in the wheelchair and there was this very big man pushing him. There was the vicar. So they lifted him up and put him on the bed. Well the vicar was standing there. This is why I'm fading out... So! The vicar stood there with the Bible, reading from the Bible in his head, and I was asking God to heal this man. When I finished I wanted to say to the man and the vicar: 'Well, I'm sure God will help', and I stood back. This is what I wanted to say. That wasn't what came out of my lips. What came out of my lips was these words: 'GET UP AND WALK!' The vicar was shocked that I would say such a thing. I was even shocked that I said it! The man got up and walked ... and he walked normally. The vicar could not believe this. They all run out of the house and left the wheelchair behind. They came back and got the wheelchair, but I never heard from any of them ever again.

But I did hear, about five years after that... A man came to see me, and he says: 'I'm having some building work done at home ... and we were just talking about being sick.' And the builder relayed the story of bringing his friend to see me. He said that his friend was completely cured, and still walking around now. Now, I wished it happened for everybody. I don't know the reason why for some and not for others. I do nothing different. I love you just the same. But there are reasons, at one level, you don't want to release it yet. At this level you don't want to release [points to the I — higher mind in picture]. At this level you want to release [points to lower mind, below]. So, you have to turn it around.

You see, you are not the body ... the body is not you. The mind is not you. How can you prove that? Stop thinking. I proved that to scientists. This is what Masters do, they stop thinking. Now, if a

Master can do it, you can do it. You can do it, I promise you. The point is, do you want to do it? That's the difference. People say — you hear these Masters say — 'Have no desire.' But that's not true. Of course, when you reach a certain level, the desire drops away. But the first desire is like the swing of the pendulum. You have to start it off. Then momentum: cause and effect. You see? You understand that? It starts to swing, then the desire automatically drops away.

To get to the stage of *Is-ness*, there has to be no desire. Because you cannot get to it, you are it. You are it! See, you can desire bliss and you can move into it and it's beautiful, but don't get stuck there. Because that can also be negative. Because you can desire it, so it can then be interpreted as negativity. You know, once you are into that state of bliss, you have to be very careful of inertia. No movement. Now, where can you go from bliss? The next stage, which is not a stage, is *beingness* ... or *Is-ness*.

Now, what's the time? It's time — exactly. Okay, in a moment we're going to have some lunch — well you're going have some lunch. Are there any questions on what we have been talking about at the moment? She has a question: stand up!

MEMBER OF AUDIENCE: *You were talking about Father, Son and Holy Ghost. What about Mother Mary, the female principle?*

STEPHEN: No, no, no, let's not get into this you and me business — of male and female — because ... let me explain to you. Yeah, let me explain to you. There is only one male in existence ... we are all female. All of us are female before we take on a gender. We are sexless. What decides if we are male or female — you call it genetics. But genetics is covered by a law of karma. There has to be a matrix. This matrix, I have to talk about it at a much deeper level, not here ... Now, in Hinduism there is only one male in existence, that's the conscious force. Divine Mother is the creative principle ... The Holy Ghost. You see, we have the Father, the Son and the Holy Ghost. I know where you are coming from, I understand that. I love the divine Mother very much.

Let me tell you a quick story: very recently I was working in the surgery in England, and there's a patient on the bed. I have a big white towel on the patient. As I am working, I notice the room turning pink. So I went outside and I asked the helper to come in. I said: 'What can you see?' She said: 'Everything is turning pink!' She went out, and I continued working. Then the divine Mother appeared, and she put her hand on the towel and rested it there. When she took her hand off the towel, her hand print in pink was left on the towel. I have the towel in the surgery; when you hold it up to the light, you see the hand of the divine mother. And when I put my hand against it, her hand is much bigger than mine. And there were several witnesses to it that day. So if the question is: do I love the divine Mother? I love the divine Mother very much! Do I see any difference between male and female: no, I don't. Is God male or female? I don't get into politics. I tell you as it is.

I began by telling you I think women are very strong. I think you have got to deserve being a woman in different lifetimes. That's what I believe. I have great respect for women, for your strength, not for your weakness, because even men have weaknesses! I don't love you for your weaknesses; well, I love all of you of course, but I respect your strengths. So, the hand print is still on the big white towel, and now when the divine Mother comes to me, I remember when...

There were several people sitting in the front, and I said the divine mother is coming ... and as she came, they filmed me. And you can see the divine mother coming over me here, the pink. This is how I got the name of the Pink Swami... Because it started off many years ago. After I was working with patients I would wash my hands in cold water, and the water would turn pink. So, I thought: 'This is very strange.' Then, when I showered, the water would hit me and turn pink. Then my white clothes started to turn pink, then the bed ... white sheets would turn pink. Very beautiful. And this would happen even with men's shirts: they would turn pink, even the buttons would turn pink and stay pink. See, just love, love, love.

Love is God, God is love. You are God, you are love. We are all flowers in the garden of God. Some are big, some are small, some are fat, some are skinny, but they all go to make the garden of God. But we are all connected to the same root system, the creative principle – a matrix governed by consciousness. I hope I've answered your question.

MEMBER OF AUDIENCE: *I just meant that there are different energies.*

STEPHEN: No, but you see what I am saying – in truth there is only one energy. There's only one energy, but we create this... You know, the Father is strong. I am the male energy, I am Shiva: whhooooaah. Rrrrraaaaa! Or, I am the divine Mother energy: soft, loving. You see, some people cannot take the strength of the Father, because the Father is hard, so they prefer to worship the Mother, soft. So God is giving you what you want. In other words, you are giving yourself what you want. You are attracting what is alike with your magnetism. I think we'll have to stop there ... okay?

You know, I love Jesus very much – you know why? Because he turned the water into wine... Thank you, Jesus. He's my hero! Just think, he could have turned the wine into water. Wow. You know, you notice these great Masters; they *play* – that's called *Lila.*[*] They are plays of God. They know how to play the game. Now, try to set your mind back 2,000 years. Jesus was at a wedding: he sat there, and maybe one of the disciples, or maybe Mary, who knows, came up to him and said, 'Oh J.C., they've run out of wine here. What are you going to do?' 'Oh no ... don't bother me!' And maybe Mary said to the guests, 'Don't worry he will do something!' And maybe Mary says, 'Eh J.C. ... do something!' And J.C. may have said, 'Even before you ask, God has given it to you! Look in the pots, look in the water pots!' So they go, 'Ahh, this is not water this is wine!'

Can you see the play? Was there a great fuss about what he did? Did he go: 'OH TURN INTO WINE!!!'? No, he knew. This is the greatness of such a soul as Jesus. He knew. There was no doubt in

---

[*] Sanskrit, meaning 'the divine play'.

his mind that this would not happen. No doubt. He had perfect concentration... Perfect faith... Matter of fact, he had 100% faith in God, and he had 100% confidence in God – 100% faith in God means he knows God is there; 100% confidence in God means, in the Word of God. He knew what came from his lips could not be a lie. So, he had 100% faith in God and 100% confidence in God. Now, that made 200% devotion to God! How could he go wrong?

Look, I notice some of you chewing gum. You know, if you were to repeat the name of God the amount of times you chew chewing gum, you would get God realization very quickly. It's true. It's so simple to have bad habits, but why is it so hard to have good ones? It's so simple to lie – why is it so hard to tell the truth? And you know, inside of you, everybody wants to live the truth! But we have created a culture of liars. How can a society based on truth survive? Can you imagine your President telling you the truth? Wow... Or, an MP? Telling you the truth? They tell you what you want to hear. Because if you tell the truth, you'll be on the cross. They will crucify you. But you know, what they don't understand... A society that is built on untruth cannot survive, will not survive; it will change into something else, and that something else can be good or bad. It's all according to what you want. How do you want to live your life? What do you want from it?

I come back to: Love sets you free. Can you think of a member of parliament being in truth and giving in honour of the people he represents? It's human nature to evolve, to grow, to expand. God is the process ... and the process is life. Because there is a matrix within the process, life will always survive. Even if all this universe explodes and physical life as you know it disappears. There will be another universe, another expression of that life. It can't be any other way. That's how it's been created. And don't think it's been going on only for billions of years. It's been going on for eternity. To understand eternity, you have to live forever.

What's the difference between forever and eternity? You are eternal, you are forever. But look, you can't even live for 40, 50, 60,

70 years on this planet. You're fed up with it. You're tired of it. You're angry. Say God said to you right this moment – say I said to you: 'Okay, you have this body forever now, this is it'. Some of you would go running out of here pulling your hair out and screaming. And you only live 50, 60, 70 years. What's it going to be like when you realize you are eternal? Your mind can't take it. That's one of the reasons why you come back. In other words, you fall asleep from the ultimate reality, because you are not at an evolutionary stage where you can accept *forever* – you can't even accept *now* let alone *forever*.

This is why it's important to train yourself, to become the master of your mind, to become the master of your destiny. Destiny is like a train ride. Sometimes the train has to stop and you have to get off and look around. It's very beautiful; life is like that. Life is like a journey, but where do you come from and where do you go? You come from yourself and you go back to yourself. For there is nowhere to go. God is forever. You have never died. Because in truth, you have never lived. You are – you're all there is. Hard concept, huh?

I bet you don't feel much like God, do you? In your higher states of awareness, yes: you may feel like it when you are in nature, when you are in love, you feel like God. But when you are angry and you're in fear, you feel more like the devil. You see, the devil and God are not separate. It's the same thing, but it's here [points to head]. It's the lower and the higher mind. It's where you decide to live. It's all it is: the line, one step. Are you ready to make the step? Do you want to make the step? If you want to make the step, make the step, decide to do it! You see, the difference between you and a Master is that once the Master has decided what he wants, he does not change his mind. What some of you want today, you don't want tomorrow, do you? But the Masters don't work that way.

The Master's willpower ... He sees God as the target, his mind is the bow because it bends, his willpower is the string on the bow, his thought is the arrow. And the target is God. And God is too big to miss. You cannot miss God, it's impossible – even if you don't know how to shoot an arrow. But you see, the Master doesn't change his mind, or her mind. They empower themselves. Like a good business man, they empower themselves. This is why I say to you, take back your *power*. Say: 'Yes, God.' In other words, you are saying *yes* to the self, but you have to bring that into your life. You have to bring it into the heart.

You see, the heart is like a dark cave; the cave can be dark for a million years, but the moment you put a light into it, the darkness runs away. Put the light of God into your heart. Let the darkness of fear run away. I promise you, you will live a life that will be so wonderful, that you will feel a freedom that you have not felt before; that you will feel a love that, wow, will blow your brains out! A love that never says *no* to you. A love that only says *yes, yes, yes*. I don't ask you to take my word for it; I ask you to experience it for yourself. To say yes to yourself ... to empower yourself. To live the life you really – in your heart – want to live. Come back to who you really are, not what the mind has made you into. The uncontrolled mind makes us into monsters. It does not make us into lovers. Decide what do you want. It's your choice. It's our choice.

Right, now we're going to talk about *dis-at-ease*. If you look at the word disease, and you break it up, you'll see it's dis-ease, dis-at-ease, *so* what is dis-at-ease? Well, we are! What is we, because it's plural? It means more than one of us. And we know we are a tri-part person, which is the Father, Son and Holy Ghost. So we have outer bodies. These outer bodies are called sheaths. The first body you will see is called the etheric body. Or, they call it maybe the body of light. We need to talk about this.

Now, before I do that... Who's tired? You are tired? Stand up! [They do jumping exercises.] Come on, come on. Are you still tired? Yes? Okay, come on then! [More exercises.] Are you still tired? No? Who else is tired? You know, okay ... I'll talk about this in a moment.

What gives us life? Breathing... Now, God is the process... So, you breathe, and a process takes place... What are you breathing in? Oxygen. Okay. What is in the oxygen? The Masters call it *prana*. What is prana? Well, if you see it, and many people ... I can see it. It's like very small particles of light dancing. These are particles of charged, positive and negative energy. I'm not going to look into it too deeply because maybe we'll do another seminar on Creation. But these charged particles, when you take them in... First of all, these charged particles are like miniature time bombs. You take them in and as they come into the lung, they explode. The electricity is withdrawn from the particle; this electricity goes into 72,000 astral nerves, and there's always a little left over of the electricity; it goes into the collective. Where is the collective? Or the storehouse? In the base chakra [points to coccyx]. You call it the *Kundalini*.

Kundalini is pure electricity, raw electricity. And a lot of people get mixed up with this, because they raise the Kundalini and they see the light. And they think they've reached God. They are lost in their truth. So the biproduct of the electricity feeds the Kundalini. Now, once the particle enters the lung and the explosion takes place, the biproduct of the particle comes out as carbon dioxide. Can you see the perfect balance of God now? Because what do trees live on? Carbon dioxide – they take in carbon dioxide. And what do they give off? Oxygen. So, you are destroying your own environment by cutting the trees down. You are killing yourselves. Out of stupidity. Out of greed. You are so insensitive that you are destroying the harmony that has been created for us to survive on this planet. You see, so all of nature, including us, is a part of the process. Everything depends on everything else.

How long do you think you would survive if there was no sunlight? How long are you going to survive if there's no rain? How long are you going to survive when all the trees have gone? How long are you going to survive when you've poisoned all of the oceans? How long are you going to survive when you've poisoned all of the land? How long are you going to survive when you've poisoned your own mind? Where is the survival instinct? You say *yes* for all the wrong reasons... Where is your courage? Where is your strength to get up and say; 'This is it!' See, your very breath is life.

Now, when we do this, we are going to do what we call seminar one ... which I have called the Creation. I will show you how you can stop breathing. Don't worry, you won't die. No, you won't die; most of you are dead already but you don't realize it! You just don't lay down. If this is living...? Okay, so what happens when this electricity goes in? Now, this is my drawing of a cell of the body. Now remember, you have billions and billions of these. It's like a little fine hair of life that comes from a battery that is charged. Now, if you can imagine billions of these cells together, what will you get? You get light, and this is called the *etheric* light.

One of the things that will destroy a cell – remember the cells are changing all the time; they die off, new ones happen – but when there is a disease, the place it affects first is the body of light. We're going to do an experiment, and we're going to do a little meditation together. You see, when you are in love, you expand, because love sets you free. But when you are in fear, you contract. This is what fear and love do. So, we're going to do a little meditation, and we're going to breathe. We're going to breathe through our mouth. As we breathe in, we're going to say *Yes*, and as we breathe out, *God*. So it's simple. You're going to close your eyes, you're going to breathe nice and deep through the mouth. As you breathe in you'll say *Yes*, and as you breathe out, *God*. But close your eyes as you do this, and open your mouth; make sure the breath is deep. Remember you are answering God. Reach out to God. Stretch your mind out. You are speaking with God. God is answering you. Exercise for a few minutes... [Claps hands loudly and people jump.]

Okay, what happened? You imploded, you feel shock. The body of light was stretching out, shock came and *pow*! Now try to imagine this happening every day. It may only be small, little shocks, the same type of shock over and over again – and every time your body of light is pulling in. But it's pulling in unconsciously. In other words, that is negative energy that is building up in your body of light. Now, this negative energy has to go somewhere. Right now it's in the body of light. But if you continue to have just a small bit...

Okay, there's the body of light. Now, these little shocks bring a reaction. Let's just say that the reaction is down here. So, because the body is holding the negative energy, the first thing that happens is that the cells just switch off. So, the light from the cell is no more. So that place where that negative energy is, is manifesting from the unseen into the seen. It has nowhere to go, except to manifest in the body. So, from the outer body to the inner body. It will manifest possibly as a tumour, because of condensed light. Remember, you are of light. The light is becoming condensed because of negativity. The intensity of that negativity has to out-birth itself, and the only place it can out-birth itself is in the physical body, as disease. It manifested first in the etheric body and condensed down, out-birthing itself into the physical body. As disease, it has to manifest itself. Of course, there's a lot more in it than just shock or fear. It could be a part of your karma, your past karma. So this is just a part of the surface that we are talking about. But you can see what has happened when you were meditating. You expanded out, shock came, there was an implosion, the body of light collapsed. And you felt weak. So there's ways of empowering yourself to make you strong; there's ways of disempowering yourself...

You are a strong person? You are strong? He's a strong man. Go like this, put your resistance against me ... [pushes down on audience member's hand] Yeah, that's strong. Now, if I want to disempower him ... [suddenly hits him in the stomach and pushes down on his arm, which now gives way]. If I want to re-empower him ... [puts hand on stomach and moves upwards, then puts pressure on his arm again and it holds strong]. I'm putting the same pressure again. What I did was to take his power. I disempowered him. It doesn't matter how strong a person is. This is more stronger [points to the head]. And this is what women can use in what we call psychic self-defense, to take away your aggressive power. So, if somebody comes to fight you, in your mind, swipe them. In your mind, swipe them, keep swiping them and they will get weaker and weaker ... and that will give you time to run away. But you must never use it for anything bad. Only to protect yourself.

But the only thing I use is Jesus, and I'm not a Christian. I just think when I'm in a bad situation: 'What would Jesus do in this situation?' And the answer is always the same ... Love. That disarms me from getting angry. It may not disarm the attacker but it disarms me from getting angry and from holding that anger, and creating this kind of disease [points to the picture of the aura]. Any questions?

MEMBER OF AUDIENCE: *You were talking about the negative energy which condenses on the body of light. Is it necessary that it manifests finally in the physical body or are there other ways?*

STEPHEN: There's other ways of cleansing it, if you know it's there. Of course, the best way is to fill your body with light. How do you think I am able to dematerialize? I do it because I fill my body with light. I fill the cells of my body with so much light that they vibrate very quickly, so I become out of sight to the physical world. In other words, I become *enlightened*. I say to you this: *lighten up!* It's that simple. It's a science. It's nothing to do with religion ... It's a science of love. It's a science, it's a divine science. I told you all the way through this seminar today: 'Love sets you free.' Love does not make you a prisoner. If you are a prisoner, then ask yourself why. The answer is always the same: out of fear. Out of fear of maybe losing someone you love, or something you love. That's where it is.

Where do you want to live? What part of you do you want to express now, in this reality? How do you want to live your life now? How can we get rid of some of this? By thinking the right action first, of course. The first thing is to stop disempowering yourself, and empower yourself. Empower yourself with the love of God. What is the love of God? The love of God is Truth. So the second thing is to live the Truth. The Truth is that God is the process. Live the process consciously. Everything *is* God. You cannot escape the Truth, no more than you can escape yourself.

People say to me: 'Oh I'm going to India to find God.' Look, if you look in the mirror here, you will look at yourself. If you go to India, you'll look in the mirror; you'll see yourself. Where can you go where you are not? There is nowhere to go. When you look in the mirror, who is looking back at you? God. But I know when you look in the mirror it's not the face of God looking back at you, is it? It's the face of too much *hurry*, too much *worry* and too much *curry*! But the truth of it is God looking back at you. This is why I emphasize: 'There's nowhere to go'. God is everywhere and everything at all times. He is the three in one, the Holy Trinity. The Father, the Son and the Holy Ghost. It's true, you see.

Wow, you know, just thinking of God is so beautiful. And I know what some of you are thinking. Well, if there's a God, how does he allow so much pain in the world? I can read your thoughts [points to a member of the audience]. Yeah, I could read your thoughts. God doesn't allow anything. He doesn't care one way or another. God is the process. You are the creator. Who is creating the pain in the world? You are! Not God. You have choices. There's enough food in the world to go around to feed everybody. There's an educational system in the world that would teach how to grow food – how to live in harmony with God's Law. Think about it.

You know, let's take one country. Russia could put men on the moon, but they can't even feed their own people, and this happens in many countries, in different ways. [Robert] Mugabe chucks all the farmers out of the country [Zimbabwe], so his people are dying now of starvation, famine – and you know, it's all like this throughout the world, in every country. So, it's not what God makes of man, it's what man makes of man. Man sets himself up as God. But it's the 'ego God'. Not the God of understanding. A true King of Materialism knows he needs the Queen sitting by him. This is the Queen of Spirituality. You have to go hand in hand. Otherwise there's destruction, disharmony. So, it's not what God makes of the world.

Look, let's put it this way: Are you a mother? Would you send your child to a kindergarten school where you know the teachers would beat them? No? You send them to the kindergarten because you know it's a good place for your children. They get looked after, they get fed, it's a beautiful place, they can't get hurt. You know your child is safe. So what do you think God has given you? He's put you into a school here, a kindergarten. He's given you everything that is needed for you. For your growth. He's given you everything. Do you think God is so insensitive that he does not know? Do you think he would act any differently to the mother?

But the one thing God gave you is free will. And he will not interfere with your free will. You see, God's will is my will. But my will is not God's will. That's the difference. When you can harmonize yourself with God's will, then you will live in paradise, because when you only confirm the will of man, then you live in hell. The choice is yours. You have free will. How can an African country, that cannot feed their people and lets them die of starvation, buy guns and whisky while their people starve? See, not the will of God, but the will of man. And in each of us, we have that possibility. You know it, in your lives you've expressed it. Because you've expressed love and you've expressed hate [pretends to throttle member of audience]. You are living the same – you are no different. But hopefully, education creates a way of life that is in harmony with the process we call God. If you try to harm the process, you harm yourself. You destroy yourself. God only has love for you. But remember, his love is unconditional. So, he doesn't care one way or another. He sees you being yourself, but he also sees you growing as children.

You see, how does society grow? It grows by observation, serving, going through pain. As society grows, it goes through growing pains. You look back and you see wars, and you don't want this anymore. So hopefully, you grow from it. You learn to live in harmony with yourself ... and the process. Remember, in harmony with the self and the process means in harmony with your neighbour, because they are also part of the process, equally as you are.

What the problem is, is the fear of change. You fear change. You hold on to what you have, like a miser holds on to his money. But change has to take place. Otherwise, how do you evolve? How do you grow, if things don't change? Do you want them to change for the worst, or do you want them to change for the better? And of course, you want them to change for the better. You want to know that when you send your children out to school, they are safe; that when your women walk out at night, they are safe.

You know, like some of you in England, when I was a child, living in London, you could leave your door open. Nobody would come and pinch anything. Now they will shoot you for nothing. What they don't understand is the bad karma they are creating for themselves. But only through education can we grow. We teach about education in our schools, the education of the computer. Everybody must have a computer. But we have no education about life. How to live it? Strange that our children grow up with numbers in their brain, with computers in their brain, but not how to treat each other. And when they are taught Religious Education, it is so blind. No wonder there is pain and division in the world.

What would happen if we all realized there was only one God? That we are all the children of God? That if I harm you, I am only harming myself? What would happen? There could be a change, because you would not want to see your brother or sister harmed in any way. How can one half of the world live with so much food that you throw it in the bin, and the rest of the world are dying because of starvation? We have to address the balance. But you have to address the balance first in yourself. Then it's love, then it's the truth, and you are putting the truth into action because you are living it. 'I am the living truth', sayeth the Lord. He was telling you. Any questions now about this?

MEMBER OF AUDIENCE: *Can we heal from the etheric body to the physical body?*

STEPHEN: Yes! How? Okay . . . by drawing in light. By drawing in light. Breathing. Simply breathing. You see, you think the great Masters used some incredible techniques. The technique is quite simple. What you do is to watch the breath come in and watch the breath go out. That's all. Simple, isn't it? But of course, there's other things we can do. The idea of meditation is to make it as simple as possible. You see, some yogis tell you to concentrate on the end of your nose. This is absolutely wrong. The only thing that's going to happen is you're going to go cross-eyed, like this!

MEMBER OF AUDIENCE: *What about what sun-gazing yogis do?*

STEPHEN: There are many ways to develop your concentration and get amazing results, and this does stimulate the pineal gland, but you need training as it can be detrimental to the eyes. Do not try it without training![*] Now, if you look at the skull of a human being, you'll see that the opening of the nose is not here [plays with his nose]. This is only gristle, fat. The opening is here, just below the chakra, what you would term the third eye. So, that's where you would concentrate. So when you see the breath come in, you see it comes in from here [points to the bridge of his nose]. And when you see it go out, you see it go out from there. And there's a mantra you can use. Some of the great Masters use *So Ham*. So, as you breathe in, *So*, and as you breathe out, *Ham*. So . . . Ham . . . So . . . Ham . . . Do you know this one? So Ham, So Ham, it's a song isn't it? Play it?

So, as you breathe in *So*, and as you breathe out, *Ham*. So Ham is the place from which the outbreath expands, when consciousness and energy have united within the creative principle. The meaning is: I am That, I am He, I am God, one could say.

See how simple it is? So, what you are doing is sitting there watching the light come in, the breath come in, and the breath go out. Of course, there's a lot more in it than that, and there are much deeper exercises of breath. To reach what you call 'the fifty breaths', that's breathing in fifty times and breathing out fifty times. And of course, bringing the light in, bringing the light up, bringing the light down into the heart, and out. These are exercises only for people

---

[*] The human eye is very sensitive, and prolonged exposure to direct sunlight can lead to solar retinopathy, pterygium, cataracts and often blindness.

who are really interested in doing this. But they are very powerful. Extremely powerful. And they will change your life if you do them. But you know you have to want to do them.

We're going to do one exercise together, and we're going to just breathe in, and I'll show you what I want you to do. We're going to breathe in three breaths, pushing your stomach out. You see, a full breath is when you breathe in and your stomach comes out. It's one movement. Because most people are shallow breathers, they are only using half of their lungs. A yogi uses all of the capacity of the lungs. I'm going to show you quickly how to energize yourself, and all you need to do is . . . you can stand for this, or sit. Might be good to stand, but you can sit and do this equally as well, and what you do . . . Watch my stomach [takes three inhalations, pushes stomach out with the breath three times, and three exhalations in which he brings stomach in with the breath]. Nothing to it, is there? But you see, when I do it, I'm saying God, God, God. God, God, God. [Motions three times up and in, and down and out.] Because as I draw the prana in, by adding the name of God to the prana, I'm giving more energy to the prana. I'm doubling the energy of the prana. This is called *pranayama*. So I'm giving myself twice the amount of energy. So my body of light will expand. Try it. Close your eyes. It's better to close your eyes because you know people can distract you. Sit with your back straight. Your back in any exercise wants to be straight, and that will be explained to you in the next seminar, if you come to the next seminar!

Take those breaths! Come on, deep! Fill your lungs – come on! – with that energy, that divine energy. Let your stomach push out. Keep your mouth open. That shouldn't be hard for you. Now, take a very deep breath through the mouth, push your stomach out, another deep breath, and hold it [pauses for approx. 30 seconds]. Okay, out. That's a very simple exercise to energize your body. There's another one, but that is more hard work. I will show you that another time. But in our next seminar we are going to do a teaching seminar. We will call it Creation. How did God come to

Creation? And, how can you live your life in harmony by using techniques? But I can tell you now. The best way is just to love. That's it, to love God with the burning passion of a thousand suns!

Wow! I could tell you so many experiences I've had, so many – and you know, God is real. That's what some of you don't realize. Did you think God is so out of your reach? She is not. God is not out of your reach. He's closer than your own nose, but you're too blind to see it. Take away the curtain. Let the sunlight come in, and live it. Shall we have some music now? Because you know, I could go around and thank everybody individually, and maybe we should thank our players, we should thank the organization, and I think we should thank God.

So I'm pleased to see – because this seminar was at very short notice – so many people. And you are all beautiful people. And you know I love you. I don't care what you think of me when you go out of here. It's not mine. But I wish you well, and I wish the very best for you. Whatever God gives you in this life, say thank you to him. It doesn't matter how bad it gets, how hard it seems: Thank you, God. God will never leave you. Never. You will leave God. He will never leave you. Even in the darkest periods of your life. He is there with you, ready to hold you in his arms. To caress you. To say: 'My beloved child, I am always with you.' And this is for everybody.

Not any one person is separate from God. I know this from my own life, so what I tell, I'm speaking from my life experience. I know how close God is. When you think he's a million miles away from you, he is right in front of you. Do you remember that poem called 'Footprints in the Sand'. It is so true. It is so beautiful that when I say it, tears would just roll down my cheeks. Because it's so true, that you are never alone; that when you think you cannot walk another step and you look back and think: 'How did I walk through that period of my life . . .?' You didn't walk, you didn't run – God carried you. That's how much he loves you.

God never turns his back on you. Impossible. You can never be separate from his love. Impossible. The separation is only in your mind. The advice I can give you, if I can give you anything, is: Don't cut yourself off from the love of God. You are the Truth. Live it. Don't live it in fear. Don't even live it merely with Love... Live it with God! See the difference when you do it. When you do it and you say *yes* to God, God will say *yes* to you. You don't have to believe what I'm telling you. Experience it for yourself. If you don't like it, change it. Simple, but you can only talk from a point of experience, and you cannot have the experience until you try it. I can tell you how to drive a car, but if you've never driven one, what do you understand of it?

God bless you. Have a safe journey home.

<u>2.</u>

The Yoga Of Oneness

Very good morning everybody. Yes, good, I don't have to speak to a graveyard – that's not good. You know, I can speak to the dead, but speaking to the living is harder. Okay, you see what I wrote: 'What is the true mark of a human being? Love – Love – Love.' Can't you see at the back? Do you want to come closer? If you can't see the word Love, we will sing it together. Love is so beautiful.

What is the problem with our lives? We forgot how to love. We forgot what life is about. We go to work, to earn money, to buy food, to give us energy, to go to work, to earn money, to buy food, to give us energy, to go to work, to earn money... This is what we do. We are so caught up in this trap that we forget who we are. We spend no time on ourselves.

Remember the words of Jesus, 'And the Kingdom of Heaven is within you!' Yes, you remember. If you do not go within, you will go without! Inside is the Kingdom of God. How can you see the Kingdom of God if your eyes are not open? People walk around like this [puts fingers in his ears]. They are dead to the voice of God. And you know, you have eyes, but you are blind. What do you see? Look at your country. It is so beautiful. How can you miss God? He is too big. You know, wherever you aim, you must see the target. God is so big, you can't miss Him. Yes, it's true. You cannot even fall off this planet without God knowing about it.

What do you want from your life? You want peace; you want love, but look at you. You are not in peace, you are in pieces. You are not in love, you are in fear. You see, what do we have here? Love – fear. Of course, we know it's more complicated than just a straight line. We know that. Because we have emotions. These emotions also cause the problems in our head. This head, you know, it controls us. I spoke to you before about this head. To understand the head, you have to go back to a time before time began. We have to go to the time when we were the soul, when we were free and in love with God. The soul was in bliss. It did not understand the fear. It understood nothing except freedom. It was in the state of being-ness.

Now, it decided to take a body. When a soul takes a body, it takes two slaves. The first slave is the mind; the second slave is the body. And of course, the soul is the master. But look at you; you don't look like masters to me. You look more like slaves. What has happened? Simple, you disempowered yourself. That's what you did. And you gave your power to the mind. Now the mind is the master and you are the slave. And you chase the body like a dog. And the mind, you know, it throws the pieces of food instead, just to keep you interested. But why should you be happy with only the scraps from the table, when you can have the whole feast?

Remember the words of Jesus, 'And the Truth will set you free!' He made it so plain and so clear: 'Live the Truth! You are the living Truth of God!' But you are living in denial; you deny yourself. You are not free. You are prisoners. This is what Jesus told us. And he said to Satan,: 'Get behind me!' What did He mean? He meant the ego. He had to get his ego behind Him. Look, when you walk away from the Light, your shadow is in front of you. When you walk towards the Light, your shadow is at the back of you. The freedom is here [points to head] in just this magic word, 'Yes!' To take back your power, to reinvest in yourself, to say 'yes' to yourself. And we have to start somewhere.

So we have to change our thoughts. We have thoughts that we ourselves are not worthy beings, that we can love everybody maybe but we cannot even love ourselves. This is the biggest sin, not to love yourself. Because if you cannot love the self, you cannot love God. Because God is within you. So denying the self, you deny God. So we have to change our thought pattern. How do we do this? Well, we start in the morning; instead of getting up and saying 'Good *moaning*!' You know, I know how it looks like when you get up in the morning. You are as crazy as I am, so it's okay. Join us, it's okay to be crazy. If you're gonna be crazy, be God crazy. So, we get up in the morning, okay? Get the thought right to start with. Get up, open your window, stand in front of the window, put your hands up like this, make sure nobody is looking at you, take a nice deep breath, and shout, 'I am great!' Oh, you want to try it? Okay! Stand up! Okay clever people. It is still morning, we have time. Take a deep breath: 'I am great!' I heard nothing. 'I AM GREAT!!!'

And because we are Light condensed into this body, we can alter this body structure. This is what I do when I do surgery. This is what I do when I dematerialize. Would you like to see me disappear? Yes? No. I will stay here. Okay, I will disappear for you. But, to make this work, you must close your eyes. What? What is the matter? Only joking. You know I've had many wonderful experiences. And ninety per cent of my experiences have always been witnessed. The last time I did the dematerialization was in Israel. I was being interviewed by the national newspaper, and when they filmed me I dematerialized, and they wrote in the newspaper – it's true, I have pictures – 'A magician!' Now, you thought they would have said, 'How did you do it?' No, just magician.

Well you see, it is not magic. To do what I do is a science. It is the Science of Love. You see, if you say to me, do you believe in God? I will say, 'no!' Because there is no belief from my part. I know God exists. I don't have to believe, I know. It's simple. So, whatever I am doing, I am doing with God. When I breathe, I breathe with God. When I walk, I walk with God. When I am listening, I am listening to God. When I am looking, I am looking at God. You see, every one of you is my lover, because when I look at you, I see God looking straight back at me. There is not one place where God does not exist.

You only think you are this body. Of course you are not. The body comes and the body goes. So why should I attach too much importance to it. Respect it, keep it clean, but don't get stuck in it. Be free. Love sets you free. I told you this. When you are in love, you can fly in the air. When you are in love, you can walk on the water. When you are in love, you can turn that water into wine. You see, Jesus did it. And you know, I am so happy that He turned water into wine, not the wine into water. Thank you, Jesus, thank you, Jesus! Jesus is my Saviour. It's true, you see. He has so much Love for us; it's the same with all the great Masters.

You know, you see many of the photographs taken by people when God is speaking to me, this Light appearance... And people say, 'How has this happened?' It is through magnetism; I magnetize my *soma.** I told you, it's a science. How did this science come about? Well it came about 12,000–14,000 years ago in the country you call India. An Aryan race came and settled by the river. These settlers were today's scientists. They were called Rishis. They were the scientists of the soul. And they practiced something we call yoga, and developed the system of meditation, of exercise, of breathing; and then the success of it got to the point where they could use it to get something called self-realization. And they got to that stage of self-realization while they were able to advance themselves by many thousands of years.

You see, look at you. You may advance yourself in one lifetime 60, 70, 80, 90 years. But these yogis, they were able to advance themselves not 60, 70, 80 or 90 years, but one or two thousand years. You see, it's the evolution of your spiritual energy. How does it work? For your brain only accepts so much electricity. You cannot put ten thousand volts through here [points to the brain] when it can take only fifty. That would blow the bulb. So, by doing exercises, preparing them for meditation, they are able to develop the synaptic nerves and astral nervous system to such a degree that they would take [withstand] flames.

I have one photograph when I raised the Kundalini, what you call

---

* Body.

the fire. When you see a Master in meditation, he is always represented by a cobra over the head – the head of the cobra is always
over the head of the Master. You will see the fire coming up, coming
over, and the head of the snake. Now, of course, if you raise this
kind of energy, it's very dangerous. It can kill you, especially if you
can't control it. This is why you develop it slowly. When you finally
raise it, you see the full light. This is why we say, 'God is Light.' This
is why we say, 'God is not in your heart, you have to put God into
your heart.' This is the doorway [points to forehead]; you have to
open the door.

Now, these Rishis developed the system of magnetism that's
called yoga. What does it mean? It means union. Union with the
self. And this group of Rishis come to be known by the name they
took from the river that they were living by. And this river was the
Indus. So they took the name Hindu. This is why women wear a
little mark here [points to forehead]. It represents the Eye of
Knowledge. Where are we going with this? We can see that
acknowledging God is not enough. We have to go further than that.
Singing, praying and mantras alone will not get you to God. If you
cannot get one bit of self-realization from it, you are wasting your
time.

I told you, 'Love sets you free!' But I am not talking about the love
that you are experiencing. Because that is not Love. We have a lower
mind and a higher mind. In Hindu terms it's called *manas*. Every
day the lower mind is working in our everyday life. So, you know,
the lower mind is in control. But when you sit for meditation, you
are giving direction to the higher mind. You say to the higher mind,
'I want you to take control.' So, when you sit for meditation, the
higher mind steps in; it may step in for a few minutes, and the lower
mind looks up and says: 'Hey, what are you doing? I am in charge,
not you!'

So, he has to get back his power, because you have disempowered the lower mind and you have empowered the higher
mind. And of course, this little demon here doesn't like it. He wants

his power back. So, it starts to throw things up. Remember, he knows you. He knows you very well. He knows exactly how to get your attention. He knows what to do to bring you back. 'God, God, oh I wish I could have a smoke', for instance. This is true. You see, you cannot go straight into meditation, unless you are a Master.

There are three stages to go to meditate. The first stage is *concentration*. Without concentration you will do nothing. So, the most important thing to develop is your concentration level. I sat tests with scientists. When they measured my concentration level, it was four times that of a normal human being. So, you have to develop concentration. But concentration is not enough. What do you need for concentration? I can concentrate to lift up my arm. And I can say to myself, 'lift! lift!' but nothing is happening. Why not? Why has nothing happened? I have to put my willpower to it. So, concentration to lift my arm; I use willpower and I can lift it. Simple. So, the first stage of any meditation should be concentration with willpower. That's the first stage.

The second stage: as you start to meditate, you come into a state of *contemplation*. What is it? Let us try to give you a demonstration of what contemplation is. Let's say you start your meditation, you concentrate — the first stage before the contemplation. Now, let's just say you think of a flower. So, you see this flower in your mind. You examine the flower, every part of it. Then, when you have examined it, you go through it. Because it's only made of light particles. And when you have got to that stage, just pass through it and the flower disappears, and you go into a stage of meditation. Of course, this is early stages of meditation.

What is the true art of yoga meditation? The first is to stop thinking. And the second is to stop breathing. These are the two highest states of meditation. Breathlessness and non-thinking. Now, if you think that is impossible — no, it's not. I can do it. You can do it. Masters can do it. If they can do it, you certainly can do it. So, the difference between a Master and you is that they have that desire to do it. They don't change their mind. Most of you start something —

halfway through it you change your mind. What you want today, you don't want tomorrow. But you see, a Master doesn't do that. The Master says, 'Yes, I want God!' Mind becomes an arrow directed straight to *OM*. How do you get to that stage of non-thinking? Well, there is a nice trick.

Before I tell you, I will retell you one of the tests I sat with the scientists. They wanted to check the activity of my brain when I was meditating. So I said, 'Look, I don't meditate now. I am always in a state of meditation. One part of my brain is always saying, 'God, God, God'. Well, they said: 'You don't understand this, but we try to test your brain.' So, they showed me a computer screen and they said: 'We are interested in these four levels. The first level is beta, do it. This is everyday consciousness'. They said: 'When we check people in meditation, they go into alpha. When we check the Zen masters, they go into theta, which is like a deep sleep. The last one is delta, this is ... nobody really goes into this, unless you are in coma.'

So, they put all these wires on my head — I looked like Frankenstein. Okay, then they said: 'Do what you are doing!' So, I was talking to them, and they said: 'What are you doing?' I said: 'I am putting my mind to sleep.' They said: 'How do you do that?' I said: 'I give it a divine anesthetic! Why?' They said: 'Because you are straight into delta! And this is not possible, while you were talking to us.' So, I said to them: 'What does it mean to you?' And they said: 'Well, it means to us scientists: you are not in your body.' So I said: 'That's good! I am in my body, but my body is not in me!' You see. I am not the body.

Now, how do I do it? This is a trick. Simple. I will show you. You have a thought, you have a gap. This is how we think: you have another thought, another gap, you have another thought, another gap, another thought, another gap... What does a Master do? Extends the gap. Simple. I put myself into the gap. Just go into the gap. And you are able to do that once you develop the state of concentration. Otherwise, you don't do it. I use a technique that the

Masters use. It's called *samana mudra*, and it's the gaze. Anywhere I am I just bring my eyelids down, my eyes go up just a little, I fix my gaze, I repeat the name of God, and that's how I will stay in that state. I will not blink. And that's how I develop; this is how the Masters develop their state of concentration. In other words I become mindless. You see, when you are playing with a lower and higher mind, a Master goes through it and becomes mindless. So they stop thinking. Now, if I can do it, you certainly can.

You see, light and darkness occupy the same space; it's not a different space. How do you switch the light on? What it's like going into a darkroom? What happens when you are going to a dark room? You are afraid, because you may fall over, there may be spiders there, somebody might be waiting to get you – your imagination goes everywhere. So what do you do? You wander around in the dark, looking for the switch. And you put it on, the light comes on and you feel safe. You see everything. There is no danger, no fear, the danger has passed. What have you done? You only put the switch on. That's only what you have done. Nothing else. Everything was there: the darkness, the light, the fear and the love. You just had to separate them. And you separate it by putting the switch on.

You see, the mind is the switch. If you switch it to the left, you are in darkness, in ignorance. If you switch it to the right, there is light, love. So, the mind is the switch, God is the electricity, and the heart is the light. Switch it on. Walk in light. Why walk in darkness? Let your light shine out. You don't have to say anything to anybody, people will notice it.

You can always tell a person when they are in love. Look at their eyes. Just look at their eyes. Because the eyes are the windows of the soul. When you are in love, your eyes shine with a passion of a thousand stars. It's true. If you are in love, you know exactly what I mean. If you are not in love, then maybe you should experience it. Because it is a drug, you see. Once you had a little bite of this, once you taste the honey, one spoonful won't be enough. You want the whole pot.

Why do you think the yogis, when they are in meditation, are so happy? You know why? Because their bellies are full of honey. It is so full of honey, so full of *prema*, love. That's it. It is so simple, isn't it? So, remember: put the switch on. How do we do that? Well, it's like you have a radio. When you are looking for a station, when you move the dial, you can hear this noise, *sssssh*, and as you come closer to the radio station, the station becomes clearer. That's it. You have to come closer to the station. Closer to that realization of God. And you tune right into that station, and then energy manifests through you. It's that simple. It really is that simple. Love is simple, it is not hard. If it was hard, I could not do it. This is why I thank God for it. Remember, Jesus said, '. . . as a child! Be as a child!' When you are free, there is nothing to fear. Just to be.

I was thinking of this meditation, it is very lovely. But what are you doing with it? What does it mean to you? You go outside and you forget it. It's nice now, but in one, two months' time, what? Why are you breathing? What are you breathing? Breath is life. But what are you breathing? People call it *prana*. But to understand *prana* you have to understand the cosmos. You have to understand the creation of life. What about if I told you that light is an illusion? That the Truth is always in darkness. No movement. No sound. Just beingness. This is the Absolute. Life is a creation of the Absolute. So, let there be Light. And there was Light. And the word was with God.

What is the sound? Oooooooooooommm . . . Listen to it. How does it sound? When you are listening to it, what does it sound like? Where did you hear that sound before? When you listen to a generator start up, it makes a sound. God, the generator. Oooooooooooommm . . . The vibration . . . If there is a beginning, there has to be an end. This is called 'The day and night of Brahma' – the *in* and *out* breath.

So, what is *prana*? How is *prana* made up? It is made up the same as every living thing. Everything you see in creation is made up of five elements: earth, fire, air, water and ether. The whole of creation

is made up of these elements. They belong to the family of *tattva**
energies. Everything in creation is made of this. But there are three
other principles, three *gunas*.

Prana, if you could see it, is light particles. These particles – I
know some of you can see them; you can see them very clearly in the
ether, they seem like little bubbles. I could show you a yoga technique so that you could see them quite clearly. These are life forces.
If you say that the circle is *prana*, the carrier of *prana* is air. The four
quarters are earth, fire, water and ether. So you can see all five
elements in combination. In truth, there aren't five elements, there
are seven. What would be the other two? Positive and negative flow
of energy... All creation is made up of magnetism and electricity.
So, everything has a common thread. This is why I said that if you
listen to the sound of Om, it sounds like a generator starting up.
How does a generator work? How do you get electricity? Please,
somebody explain. There is a magnet. So, magnetism and electricity
go together.

So, when the word is with God, the word is, 'Let there be light!'
Out of darkness came light. Light did not exist until it came out of
the mouth of God. The first was sound. But this could be argued.
You can say fire was first, and from fire came sound. Someone
could say sound come first, then fire. Well, the truth is within you.
You know the truth. And this truth will set you free. You are taking
this *prana* all the time. The moment you don't take it in, your body
will physically die, unless you are a Master, of course, and you
know how to stop breathing. Oh yes, this is true, the Masters do it.
They get to a very high state of awareness. You call it *samadhi*. This
is a high state of awareness. And you could stay in that state of
breathlessness for a very long period. You see, when they stop
breathing, the lungs stop, the heart stops, because there is no
oxygen going into the body, they are creating no carbon dioxide, so
the body is not going to decay. But they can keep the body alive in

---

* A *tattvas* are governing principles of reality.

function, by keeping enough electricity in the higher brain, still making the body go.

Of course, *prana* is very important to us, because when you breathe it in, you take it into the lungs. And what happens when it goes into the lungs? These particles of positive and negative energies, in combination with the elements, are time bombs ready to explode, and they explode in your lungs. When you breathe them in, they explode, the electricity is withdrawn from them, and that electricity goes to 72,000 astral nerves, *nadis*. There is always some electricity left, and this goes into a store room of electricity. Where do you think this store room is? The coccyx.

Okay. Why the coccyx? The kundalini. The kundalini is not in the coccyx. It is about a centimetre above the anus. So, the remains of the electricity go into the kundalini. And it's this that feeds not only astral nerves, but your biological nerves. And the byproduct of the *prana* comes out as carbon dioxide. The trees are taking the carbon dioxide and give you oxygen. We are taking the oxygen and give the trees poison. Wonderful exchange. But how stupid of you when you cut the trees down, because how are you going to feed yourselves? How are you going to breathe? What are you going to breathe? You are destroying the means to life!

Now, I will show you how to make a consciousness of this breath by showing you how to breathe properly. Okay, we are going to do a very simple breathing exercise. This is the first thing that you should learn, how to breathe properly. And I tell you this: if you were to say the name of God from your heart the number of times you chew your chewing gum, you would get God-realization very quickly! Why waste your time? Why not say the name of God? It's far better for you. The only animal I see doing this [chewing] are cows in the field. It's not for human beings!

None of you breathe properly — very few of you. You are shallow breathers and you are only breathing from here, the upper parts of your lungs. You are not using all your lung power. When you breathe, you breathe from the stomach. When you breathe in, the stomach comes out. When you breathe out, your stomach comes in. Simple, isn't it? It is so important, this breath. This is what the yogis use. This is the first basic breath. Singers know it: to breathe with the stomach and use not only the upper part of the lungs. The whole lungs have to be filled. And as funny as you may think it looks, it is very effective. I will show you how in a moment. We will do a very simple exercise.

The first exercise we are going to do is just breathing. We are going to breathe from the mouth. We are just going to open our mouths and you are going to put your tongue to touch the top of the roof of the mouth, and breathe. If you do this properly, you will feel cold air going down the throat. So you just put your head back a little bit, open your mouth and you put your tongue up onto the roof and you just breathe in and out. Using your stomach, as you breathe in you push your stomach out, as you breathe out pull your stomach in. Do this four, five times, keep your mouth open. Close your eyes. Open your mouth.

This exercise clears the ear while going through the throat. How do you know if it works if you don't try it? Okay, relax now. With the outbreath, relax. Right, and that's the beginning of an exercise. I told you about breathing in *prana*, and a magnetic force of electrical positive and negative charge. I told you that by breathing this in, it affects your electrical and biological system. So we can see, breath is very, very important. Anything that stops or influences your breath is bad, such as smoking. It is not good.

What happens to the electricity? Every cell of your body is like a miniature car battery. You can have a most beautiful Rolls Royce. If the battery is not good, it won't run. Simple, isn't it? Every cell of your body has an electrical count of positive and negative flow. Because it has an electrical count, it is a force – or force of light. This comes away from the cell like a light particle or like a hair; very, very tiny. Can you imagine billions and billions of these cells all working in unity. Every time you breathe, you are charging these cells.

So, what you see is a light body. This is called the etheric body.

Now, if you are not breathing properly, and you are not getting enough electrical energy of magnetism in, these miniature lights move close to the body, so your astral body or your light body, etheric body, can be ten foot away, or it can be a half inch away – the further it is away from you, the stronger is your power. So, where is this light body? It interpenetrates the physical body. It's inside as well as outside, and it's very sensitive. This is why, when it's not in balance, in the body of light you get blockages, or stale energy if you like. It can get stuck, it won't move, and if you keep thinking the same way, you add more negative energy to it, until eventually this blockage in the light body becomes so strong that it will out-birth itself into the physical body as disease. Or, as you know, *dis at ease* = disease. This is what it is. So, we have to clear this blockage before it manifests.

So, you do it by your breathing. Fill the light body with energy. But remember, Love sets you free. When you are in love, the light body expands, when you are in fear, it contracts. I just want you for a moment to close your eyes, breathe nice and relax, through your nose in and out; follow the breath come in and follow the breath go out. Just do this for a while. [There is a loud bang.] You see what happened? It was the implosion of your light body. The light body quickly came back. It was in shock, it was in fear. So, straight away it comes back. Don't worry, it won't do you any harm. Just take a nice deep breath and let it out. Now, there is a typical show of negative strength. You were not ready for it; the light body with-drew. That is happening all day long. Sometimes the fears are only small. But it has to go somewhere.

So, where does it go? It goes into the body of light, and it builds up, and builds up, and builds up . . . until it out-births itself. And the only place it can out-birth itself is your physical body. This is why when I am doing surgery, it's on the light body. And, when I am taking [stuff] out, you can see the change of the colour of the cotton wool. So you see, fear is your enemy. But you are so used to living in fear – that is not your second nature, it's your first nature. It's not who you are, it's not the Truth. Remember the Truth sets you free? The fear keeps you where you are now, it keeps you a prisoner. You think your big intellect will get you to God? No. You can analyze the atom. Where will it end? Be like the child. That's it.

Now, I have shown you a simple exercise – how to breathe. And look at you: 'I can't wait for a smoke!' Practice this. Fill your lungs, because the lower parts of your lungs are going to be in for a big shock. They have been so dark for so long. You are going to put some light into them. How do you feel they are going to react now? Cough, cough, cough . . . [imitates a smoker]. Lovely! It is doing me good. My nerves are so much better. So you can see roughly how the body of light works, can't you?

Expansion is love, contraction is fear. It's that simple. So, what do the yogis do? They don't allow fear in. They only allow love. This is what I said to you about the honey pot – they love the taste of the honey. They take that honey all day. So, are you going to take honey today? That secret is that when you breathe, you add the name of God, because that creates much stronger magnetism. You magnetize the *prana* even more so when you breathe it in. Watch this: as you do it your sight will get light. Try to do it. As you do it your sight will get clearer. Remember, you are saying the name of God. As you breathe in, let the voice say 'God'. Hold it, and after a while breathe out. And now, if I continue like that, I would physically disappear. Because you are sucking in *prana*, extending your light body, you are becoming light. In other words, we are lighting up. Very simple.

I need somebody who will help me . . . Now, if you could see our energy field, it's about here at the moment . . . [indicates]. This is the first energy field. This is the body of light, the etheric body. The other bodies – because there are five shields, five bodies – energy field or the aura will come up here. Around here . . . It will come out several feet away from you. This is why, when we come close to a person, your aura is feeling out that person before you even touch her. We feel things. I will prove this to you. Just put your hands in the air, close your eyes, and just slowly move your fingers in the air.

You are not playing the piano, slow down. Just move the fingers, that's all. As you move them, take a deep breath in, and you will start to feel tingling in your fingertips. Can you feel it? My hand is shaking, vibrating. Can you feel it?

That's energy there; it has always been there. Now, just move your fingers around. Just move around, and you will find different intensities of energy around you. Can you feel it? Okay, let me show you another way: face your hands together. Don't touch them, just face them. And slowly bring them close together. You will feel a resistance. Do you feel a resistance? And if you look, you can play table tennis with the energies. My hands won't come together. There is a very strong resistance. I will have to use my willpower very strongly to put my hands together. That energy has always been there, you have only just become aware of it.

Okay, open your eyes. There is a way of protecting yourself as a woman, especially in case a man tries to attack. And the way to do this is to collapse his field of energy. Just to collapse his field. We do this mentally – by mentally striking at the person. I'll show you. Put your hand like this... Now, I am pushing very hard [raises the right hand of a volunteer to the horizontal position and tells her to hold his hand strongly; there is strong resistance in her hand when Stephen tries to push it down, but when he claps her in the stomach, he takes away her power and easily pushes her hand down]. But if I was to take her energy, I just hit her in the stomach, and there is no energy, it's gone. I collapsed the field of energy. Now, if I take it back [strikes twice], it's there – the power is there again.

Now I will do the same mentally. We will replace the roles here. She is the man, I am the woman. She wants to jump on me and make love to me. I don't want it, I am a virgin. This one is aggressive. As she comes close to me, I throw a thought into her solar plexus. Now watch ... [Stephen, taking power away from the 'aggressor', knocks her to the floor without difficulty.] Very simple. It's very simple to take her energy and to finish her and just walk away. But you won't have to touch physically. Run away; look back and, through a thought: 'Stop!' And that thought will hit her energy field and the body of light will collapse. Simple. And it works.

When you are in fear, it can also be positive. All these people that are heroes were cowards. They never set out to be heroes. Out of their fear, they did what they did. So you see, fear can also be positive. That's why I repeat to you: Keep balance. Keep focused. Keep self-centred. Centre yourself. Your exercise for today is to practice that breathing. Just practice: breath in, pushing your stomach out, breath out, and your stomach comes in. I know you are laughing, you think . . . but I tell you, it is very important, breath is life.

Why do we live the present and not the moment? Well, the moment doesn't exist. And why doesn't it exist? Because of time and space and light. How do we see? With the eyes. Thus it perceives light, it's focused, and there comes the image. So, it could be said that the person here in front is seeing the future, and the person at the back is seeing the past. It may only be a nanosecond, but it's happening. So, the moment for her is not the same moment for her [the other]. So, the moment does not really exist. What exists is only the present. Live the present.

Where do you live mostly? We live in our minds. Where does our mind send us? Into the past. You know, this mind of ours is so crazy. You can be happy, doing beautiful things, then the mind says, 'What makes you be happy? I don't like you being happy! We are going to have to change that! And how can we change it? Oh, I know, I will dig something up that will take your mind away from your happiness!' So, the self-punishment begins. And we pull away from happiness. You see, the mind is so clever. But you have to be cleverer than that. The only way to empower yourself is to take back the power from the mind. When you see the mind trying to achieve his negativity, say: 'No, mind!' Say, 'No, mind! No, mind!' You see? 'No – mind!'

Remember what we said yesterday? About going through the mind? Go to that state of being focused. I told you what to practice.

The meditation of the eyes being open, or the concentration. Do you remember it? Okay, let's just make sure you remember it; you are just going to do it. And the way we are going to do it is to sit comfortably; your back has to be straight. First of all you just close your eyes, then you open them to half; you put the eyelids down slightly, and you put the eyes a little up into the eyelids. Because the eyes are going up, your eyes are going towards God. As you breathe in nice and slowly, say, 'Yes, God!' And as you breathe out, 'Yes, God!' Of course, you can use any mantra. Now, you are looking at the top of your eyelids, but you could very easily look at the picture of your guru teacher – the idea is to fix the gaze. Once the gaze is fixed, don't blink. When you feel your eyes want to blink, let them blink and start again. Try to keep your eyes fixed...

Okay, you see the concentration is very important, otherwise you won't do anything. Remember what I said yesterday about the concentration and the willpower – to balance the two? You see, we are an intricate part of God. You can't get lost. It doesn't matter where you go or where you are. You can't fall off the planet wherever you are going. And don't think that this God is some abstract thing. He is everything, of course, and is very real. And you know, He listens in. He may not always answer...

Let me give you an example of this listening in. It happened one morning in the surgery. As I was working on the first patient, I said, 'God, please open my heart, so I can feel you more in my life!' It is one of those prayers, you know, that you say ... and I forgot about it. Well, in the afternoon we had a group from France waiting to come in to see me. They were standing outside the surgery, and one of them happened to look up in the sky above the surgery, and she saw something. So she pointed it out to the rest of the group. And one from the group had a polaroid camera and they took three photographs of this thing in the sky above the centre. When the pictures developed, they come running in to show me. I was so shocked I physically fell into a chair, because the morning's prayer came straight back into my mind. A door appeared in the sky. Then comes the second photo: you can see the door is open, because you can see through it. On the third one, the face of Jesus appeared. These were instant photographs, remember that. What did Jesus say? Do you remember the words of Jesus? 'Knock on the door; I will answer you! If you open the door to me, I will come in and sup with you! I am the doorway to your heart!'* See, in the morning, I said to God, 'Please, open the door to my heart!' And He was listening. And it appeared for everybody to see in the afternoon. Better than first class post!

But He did not finish there. It was a national newspaper that heard about it, and a photographer came down. And he said, 'Did God really speak to you?' I said, 'Look, I don't take these photographs, speak to the people who did them. I am just telling you what happened.' So he said to me, 'Can I take a picture of these three photographs?' 'Of course.' A few weeks later he came back to me to show me what came out of these photographs. And what do you think had happened now? A burning bush. So I said to him, 'How did God speak to Moses?' And then I said, 'Anyway, my middle name is Moses.' It is the truth. Stephen Moses Turoff. And it's a burning bush, not a flash. You can even see faces in it as well.

Your name, your fame, your wealth – you can take none of this with you. It finishes at the grave. The only thing you can take with you is your truth. Only your truth. Remember the words of Jesus, 'And the truth will set you free!' Only the truth can set you free, nothing else. And I told you yesterday, that when you go to God you will lie to Him. You know you will. What will you say to God when you have to face Him? 'God, I have done my best!' And you know that you've not done your best, or that your best is not good enough. You know it's not. You know you could do a lot better. So, straight away you tell an untruth to God. So, how could the untruth blend with the truth? It's the opposite.

* Behold, I stand at the door, and knock: if any man hear my voice, and open the door, I will come in to him, and will sup with him, and he with me. (Revelation 3:20)

So what will happen? You will come back again and again, until you realize the truth. Remember the simple words – so simple words that He told us, 'The truth will set you free!' Look at all the great teachers that are coming to this world: Krishna, Buddha, Muhammad, Jesus, Moses, Guru Nanak, Sai Baba and many others; they all come with one message, one simple message . . . And what is it? Love. Love – Love – Love. If you practice Love, you will not hate anybody, you will not be jealous of anybody.

Oh yes, I can read your minds. You will not want to harm – not even a fly. This non-harming, *ahimsa*[*] . . . But you see, people who practice this – most people don't practice it right. They think it's only: no harming to animals. But you know, your thoughts – if you are thinking one bad thought about somebody, that is *himsa*.[†] If you wash yourself, that is *himsa*, because you are killing bacteria. You are still taking life. Even if you eat grass, you are still taking life. Don't make excuses. All life belongs to God. The same as all life responds to love.

Before you eat your food you say a prayer on it. Because the food is dead. There is nothing in it. So when you say a prayer on it, you put energy into it. You re-energize your food. Then, when that food goes into you, the energy goes into the system. And of course, that energy evolves. Energy is always evolving. What you eat evolves. Everything is evolving. But where is it evolving to? Where does it come from? Well, the answer is so clear; it's clearer than your nose on your face. It can only come from one place – that is, no place.

You think you are on the pathway to God? You are not. There is no pathway to God! Of course not, how can you be on a pathway? Why is there no pathway? Because you are already there! You are not separate from God, you only think you are. I have come to give you this message. I and the Father are One. We are One. We are not separate. We only think we are separate. But we are not. This is the

---

[*] Respect for all living things and avoidance of violence towards others.
[†] To injure or harm.

wonderful game of *maya shakti*. We are One. You are me and I am you. When I speak to you, I speak to myself. When I look at you, I look at myself. How can I see anything different than me? For I am all there is. It is nothing else. I don't see myself separate from the source. I am the source. We only have to realize it. That's what evolution is about.

The light within us is evolving. Even animals ... everything is evolving. We have come from all these stages of elements, of rock formation, ground formation, animal formation... This light within you has gone through all that. Now you are nearly at the pinnacle. Let me try to show you this — very simple. Within an animal there is about fifteen to twenty per cent of *atmic* light. Within a human being there is eighty per cent. You see, animals have group souls. When their group souls go through a stage of evolution, it will out-birth itself into a human. And from the human out-birth, it becomes individual: to be able to say, 'I am!' Although you would not think we are different from animals at all — we behave worse than animals.

What do we mean by 'being truthful'? By being truthful, you can live without sin.

Let me tell you about Jesus, what happened one day. Jesus was going to Jerusalem. And he came across the crowd of people. And he could hear them shouting, 'Stone the prostitute! Stone her! Kill the prostitute!' Jesus heard this, made his way through the crowd of people, stood in front of the prostitute, picked up the stone and he said, 'All those without sin, cast the first stone!' And it went silent. Everybody dropped their stones except one. And in the silence you could hear the sound of the stone. And the stone hit the prostitute, and she fell down. Jesus was so angry, he went through the crowd to where the stone came from, and he saw this old lady and he said to her, 'Mother, why!?' The mother was without sin. It was his mother. All those are with sin, but the mother is without sin...

But you see, what is this sin? What is it? When you are born, you are born in sin. A little baby, two or three years old, four years old, walking around . . . What is natural for the child? To touch itself. We have all done it; but when the parent sees it, it's: 'Don't do that! You mustn't do that! It is sinful!' And the baby is in shock. So, it starts to realize there is something called sin. And as the child grows up and goes to work: if it goes to work it's okay, but if it doesn't go to work, it's sinful. If you go to work and you earn money it is okay, but if you earn too much money, it's sinful.

Let us go a step further: you go to church – it's okay, but if you go to the wrong church, it's sinful. And if you die before you have confessed your sins, you just won't get into heaven. We have this inbuilt thing about sin. You see, we have to disempower it. Even our children grow up into us. Look at yourself. How you are living your life? Does your past affect you? Why do you think you don't like yourself so much? Why is it you can't love yourself? That you can love other people, but you can't love yourself? That you feel like you are in sin? It's here, in your conscience. It weighs very heavy. And we carry it around with us.

And you know, eventually the weight of our sin gets so heavy that we go like this . . . Get rid of your sins by realizing that you are not in sin! That you should be in love, not in sin! As a matter of fact, it is a sin not to be in love. I would say that the only sin in this world is not to be in love. They say: 'Well, you know, we had the first sin! From Adam and Eve, when Eve ate that apple!' Well, I am going to say only one thing about that: 'Thank you, Eve! Thank you, Eve! Thank you, thank you, thank you, Eve!' Because without Eve eating the apple, I would not be here; I would not be here experiencing God. So thank you, Adam, thank you, Eve. They are my heroes. I love them. They gave me life. They gave me experience. They gave me love.

To experience love is to experience God. Experience in love is to experience myself. So there is no sin, only the sin not to love. That is the thought of the devil. It turned it around, the devil being the ego. Turn it around. You see, you have to play the game, but all games have rules. Know the rules in this game. And it's fun. We are all actors and actresses on the stage of life. Lifetime by lifetime we play a new role. We put a new mask on. But now and again, we must sit down quietly and listen to the producer. Speak with the producer; he is not so far away from you. You see, God wants what you want. God's will is my will. But my will is not God's will. That's the difference. God only wants what we want; we are creating our reality from moment to moment. And if you don't like it, change your thought. Change it. It's that simple.

But some of you say, 'You have not got *my* body!' But you are not the body. Your body will come and your body will go. You know, you can't even believe how many times you have done it . . . Since evolution began. To this point of evolution, you have been here millions of times. Not once or twice. It doesn't end. You are eternal. There is nowhere to go; there is nothing to do, except to be. You are who you are, you can't change it. You created the game. The game goes on and on and on . . .

And yet I can sense some of your minds. Of course you are not even listening to me, because your mind is taking you away. It is always the same when people have to face the truth; the old person of Satan gets in the way. The ego won't let him see the truth. So, they will continue to suffer and won't know how to play the game. There will come a time when they will want to speak with God, but will God want to speak to them? I can see the light of every one of you; I know in what stage of evolution you are. And silently I am trying to help you. I am placing things into your energy field that will help you.

Let me tell you my experience a few weeks ago in Spain. I went into meditation and the first thing I saw straight away was a pink crystal. The crystal turned into a pink rose and opened up with pink light coming out. And when that pink rose disappeared, there was a brilliant gold light, just pulsing. I couldn't explain the beauty of this crystal rose, but it was crystal, pure crystal. Pink plays a very important part in my life. It started several years ago. After I saw a patient I washed my hands, and as I washed my hands the water turned pink. So, I thought I have something on my hands. But all that day, every time I washed my hands, the water turned pink. Then I noticed the next day when I showered, as the water came, it turned pink. So I thought, maybe it's just soap or something. Then my clothes started to turn pink. I said to my wife, 'What are you washing my whites with? They have changed colour!' And she said, 'No, I haven't put anything in.' Then the white bed sheets turned pink. Then you could see pink light coming out of my hands.

I was working in Hong Kong in a very big hall. And they had beds everywhere; they had white sheets around the beds. And the moment we had finished, all the sheets were pink. One woman came back to me and she said, 'Look, I have to show you this; I brought my daughter here yesterday and she had a white headscarf which I want to show you.' And it was pink; and it had big pink patches on it, like somebody painted it with a paint brush. And the last time this happened was in Ireland. A man came to see me. He had a white shirt on, and the next day he came to see me, because we were doing the seminar, and he said, 'Look!' He brought the shirt with him to show everybody: the shirt turned pink and even the buttons turned pink. It stayed pink. Beautiful! So, that's how I got the name Pink Swami. But my spiritual name is Prema Ananda, which means Love in Bliss. But I don't care what you call me, I will answer to everything. I am like a dog. I come back for more.

Wasting time is God wasting. You can lend money to people and you get that money back. But you cannot get time back. Marching ever towards the grave, the last breath out of your lips should be his name. I ask only two things from God. The first thing is that when I die, his name is on my lips. The second thing: when I have to come back to this world, his name is on my lips. All the rest does not matter.

I am the happiest man to be here with such beautiful people; to be with you and to have this privilege – to listen to such beautiful music. What more could I ask for? Every man should be exactly as I am. But you know, there is no luck. God always gives you what you need, not what you want. When you say 'yes' to God, you give everything to him. That means, when you walk out that door, you don't take it back. You keep it with God. He knows exactly your life – he knows it.

No Master had it easy. Muhammad, peace be upon him, said, 'I am a messenger!' And he gave the message of love. Jesus first said, 'I am the messenger of God!' And as he came to a realization, he said, 'I am the Son of God!' And as he came to realize God more, he said, 'I and the Father are one!' – that we are all the same. He made a conscious effort; he said 'no' to his monkey mind, he said 'no' to the ego. He wanted the light. He wanted his father, his mother, his best friend, his lover – this is God for him. Everything was God for him.

Do you think Jesus was some pushover like that? No, he was not. If you think Masters could not get angry, you are mistaken. If you ever heard Jesus when he was angry...! My God he was angry! Especially when he chucked the men, the money-lenders out. He was angry! Moses, when he came down from the mountain with the Ten Commandments, and he saw the chosen people, bowing before statues of animals, he took the Ten Commandments above his head and he threw it on them. 'You don't deserve them!' God gave you the Commandments... And they smashed. Muhammad, peace be upon him, went to war, because they tried to kill him because he was a radical. Every teacher was a radical. They suffered; they suffered because of the ignorance of men...

Where do all these rules and regulations come from? Of course, they come from the society. How does the society grow? It grows from observation. We observe and if we don't like something, we change it. On the way, we are making all these rules of how to live. We have made so many rules of how to live, we have forgotten to live. We only know about the rules. Don't do this, don't do that, don't do something else. My God, my head is full of rules. Well, I think if you are just a good human being... Practice being a human *being*.

People say, 'We belong to mankind.' Man is *not* kind! You have just barely reached the human stage. From this stage the man becomes kind. Are you kind? Are you kind . . .? Are you? Would you like me to tell you about your life? Would you like, in front of these people, to tell you what you have done? No, you are not kind. You have not been kind to yourself. I know. I can read you. I know. There is nothing I don't know about you. So, don't lie! Love!

Kindness starts with yourself. Don't try to change the world. Change yourself. Be kind to yourself. We have this little – unknown – muscle in ourselves, a muscle that we hardly ever use. It's called the 'letting go' muscle. Build this muscle up, and start to let go of things. Be kind to yourself. That is the first thing you should be, because your body responds to it. Your body is a living organism. And be careful with that word because there is another word very close to it. I am dyslexic . . . I can hardly say it!

Be free. Be free with yourself. Don't be a miser to yourself. Fill yourself with love. Fill yourself with light. There is so much light for you. There is so much love for you. Why do you fear it? There is no reason to fear. When you walk in the light of God, nothing can hurt you. Nothing can touch you. There is only one thing to fear: fear itself. There is nothing to fear. Be free. Be love. Be compassion. Be yourself.

They say when you die people see themselves going through a tunnel of light. Have you heard of that? They go through a tunnel and then the other world comes into focus. So, what happens? I will tell you. You are born into this world by the umbilical cord; this connects you to your mother. But when you die, you have another body; the body is called an astral body. It's a new birth. You are going to shake off this old body and you are going to take on this body. So, there is another cord, it's called the cord of light, and it's connected here [points to forehead]. So, as the spirit comes out of the body, or we say the consciousness, it withdraws through this cord. This cord is like a tunnel. So, you are feeling like you are going through a tunnel. The light at the end of the tunnel is the etheric eyes. As your consciousness makes use of the astral brain, the astral eyes start to focus, and so you begin to see the light. When that totally takes you, this cord is *kaput*. And then you are an inhabitant of the astral world.

You possibly will look round and see this body lying in its bed. Now, are you alone? No. Generally somebody will be there to meet you. It will be somebody familiar; somebody that you loved, that you trusted. Because what good is it if somebody says to you, 'Hey!' You are going to be in horror. You will be in fear. It will be somebody you trust. And they will say, 'Come on, I have to get you away from here!' And you will be quite delirious, because you will ask yourself, 'How can I be dead? I can see! I can hear! I can breathe! How can I be dead? It's impossible, I can't be dead! I can't be dead, it's impossible!' And your loved ones will say, 'Yes, come, you have passed over!' And they will say, 'You must go away from these vibrations!' And they will take you away. They will just put their arm around you like this; they will tell you to close your eyes, you will feel a rushing movement, and they will take their hand away from your eyes; you will open your eyes and you will be in a place of great beauty.

And you will need time to settle down, to adjust. If this is happening to a child, and there is no parent on the other side to meet them, the child is taken immediately to the sphere of children. I've been there. And let me tell you, it's very, very beautiful. There is a system — of course there is. There is a system where children are looked after; they are educated, of course. You still have to have an education. But they are educated more in ways of spirit than the material aspects. And they are assigned to a helper. Generally it's a woman, because of the compassionate side of women. And as the child gets to understand, they will bring the child to see the parents on the Earth. Just to be with them. This is why sometimes, when the parent loses a child — a young child — you can feel them touch you. Or say, 'Mum, mum, I am okay! I love you, mummy!' And you know all different things happen, and I've had many wonderful experiences with this. Of course, it is a little bit more complicated — this is the simple version of it.

Sometimes you can go out of your body very quickly, by an accident, or somebody can shoot you. And sometimes these souls, you know, they even don't know they are dead; they can't accept the death. Because you see, they are feeling so real. They are so 'solid'; they are doing their breathing, they are being... So, they cannot accept that they have passed over. So there are groups of people who come to these souls and tell them, 'Come, let us help you!' These are called rescuers. And you will always find this happen in battlefields, where people just can't believe they died in the battle. I wrote a book called *Seven Steps to Eternity*, and this was about a First World War soldier who communicated his life to me of how he died in the battle of the Somme; how he was rescued, his life on the other side, and how he met his parents.

People tell you to meditate in all different ways. Meditation should be easy, it should not be hard. You should control your mind. In controlling the mind you control the imagination. If you go into meditation and you only use your usual imagination, the mind has you. The mind will give you what you desire [in order to] hold you. There is only one way to meditate – stop thinking. It's the only way; otherwise you are still a slave of the mind.

So, what is the simplest way? Meditation *Sohum*.* The great Masters don't use *Sohum*. They use *Ham So*. But, we are not going to do that. We will only do *Sohum*. Why? Because at night, when you are breathing through the nostrils, you make the sound 'so', and when you breathe out, the noise from your body is 'hum'. Listen, 'Sooooo-hummmmm, sooooo-hummmmm...' And it slowly goes to 'Om'. So, at night you pronounce the name of God, *Sohum*, 'I am He'. But even that is a duality.

All the Masters are saying is to watch the breath come in and go out. But where do you watch the breath? People say, 'at the nose'. This is not correct. There is no chakra here. The only thing that is

---

*A Hindu mantra, meaning 'I am He/That' in Sanskrit. In Vedic philosophy it means identifying oneself with the universe or ultimate reality.

going to happen if you concentrate on the top of your nose is that your eyes will become crossed like this! It is the only thing. It serves no purpose whatsoever. If you look at the skeleton of the human being, where is the nose? It's not there. This is only skin and muscles. You have two holes here [points between the nose and the eyes], that's where it is. Just below, what you termed the third eye. So, this is where the Masters concentrate. And it's so simple; all that they are going to do is bring the breath in – and then they are going to watch the breath coming in; and as it comes in, they say, 'Soooooo...' They will still be in their mind. And then out, 'Huuuuuum...' That's all.

Let your mind be concentrated on that point. Breathe in the life force, and out. Some of you may see the light coming in, and the light coming out. But it must be fixed on the breath. You do not force it in any way. What happens when you do this and you master it? The in-breath cancels the out-breath out, so you stop breathing. That is the height of samadhi.* And it is as simple as that, no magic in this. Let's try it.

What is the best thing to do for good meditation, for a beginner? Well, you need the clothes to be nice and relaxing. And it's good to get a set of clothes that you take off after your meditation. So, the Indian stuff is very good, because it is very free – because when you are doing this meditation you are drawing on higher magnetic, electrical forces. So this magnetism will stay in your clothes. So when you are finished meditating, you can take the clothes off and put them in a plastic bag and put them away. So that when you put on your clothes again for meditation, they get you straight into that mood. Of course, when you are a Master, you don't need to do this.

Try to be somewhere quiet, because of the distractions. Very simple. Let's close our eyes. Keep your back straight, because the energy is flowing up the back. As you breathe in, 'Sooo!' And as you breathe out, 'Huuum!' But in your own time – no race. Your eyes

---

* State of meditative consciousness.

must be closed. Concentrate at the forehead level . . . 'Sooo-hummm, sooo-hummm, sooo-hummm. You-and-I-are-one. Soo-hummm, so-hummm, you-and-I-are-one.' Relax. And this should be practiced as much as you can. There is no time for meditation, all time is good. But early morning, about three o'clock, four o'clock, is the best. Don't shout. Don't drink anything cold. If you are going to drink anything, drink warm water. Not too much, just a few sips. And if you can't do it this way, give yourself some time. Maybe half an hour in the evening. Set a time. Say, 'This is my time!' Get the body used to that time. Practice this *So-hum*. Take the breath in, and the breath out. This is the first simple stage. This particular meditation, if you practice it and do it right, is very powerful.

If a person is having a heart attack, you lay her down; if she is still with us, of course, put the finger on the right nostril, and you let them breathe in through the left one. It's that simple. So you see, when you are doing *pranayama*[*] exercises, it's good to do it too when the mind is a bit unbalanced and you want to go to sleep. Just cover the right nostril and breathe deeply through the left, in and out through the nostril.

Now, how can we balance the body? That's so simple. We just cover the right nostril, we breathe in through the left nostril like this, nice and deep, and as you breathe deep, count to four in your mind. So, by the time you go to four you have a full breath. Hold your breath for eight, change of nostrils, let the breath come out of a right nostril for sixteen. So, you regulate the breath coming out for the count of sixteen. Pause just for a moment and breathe in through the right nostril to the count of four. Hold the breath for eight, change over nostrils to left, and breathe out through the left nostril and count to sixteen. So, it's 4-8-16. Breathe in, let's say 8, hold your breath for 16, breathe out for 32. And breathe in for 24, hold your breath for 48, exhale for 96.

Now, some of you are a little bit tired, I think. I am going to show

---

[*] Breathing.

you an exercise. I am going to take a real nice breath in through my mouth. I am going to hold my breath, I am going to bend my knees, I am going to put my hands like this [holds them forward and makes fists], and I am going to tense my body, every muscle – from my toes, up to my legs, in my buttocks, in my back, in my hands, in my face, still holding my breath … and relax. Take a nice deep breath, the breath is essential. Take a deep breath through the lungs, hold the breath, bend the legs, tighten the whole body, hold it, hold it …

Stand up! Take a deep breath, hold it, bend your legs, tense fists, tense up all your muscles, nice and tight, come on, close your eyes, everything should be tight. Hold it, hold it, hold it, hold it, out! Let's do it again. Nice deep breath, bend your legs, tighten your hands, close your eyes. Tight! Tight! Hold it! Hold it! Hold it! Hold it! Hold it! Hold it! Yes! Stretch out hands and jump a little! After this exercise you go easily into a meditation. It is so simple! The most important exercise is *So-hum*. It's not hard, it's not magic, you are not going to see anything. Hold your imagination, watch the breath come in, and watch the breath come out. Sooo-Huuum. Don't straighten anything. If there is a moment you feel any pressure that is unnatural to you, you will lose your concentration. Just gently breathe in, pause a moment, and gently breathe out. As you are practicing it more, it will become a drug to you. The most beautiful drug. Give yourself time to do it.

So, if you ask me the best method of meditation for somebody who is starting, this exercise is the real one that I showed you. And the concentration. You can practice concentration anywhere, at any time [closes eyes and concentrates]. How long would you like me to stay like this? There is no time, and I have not blinked. I could stay like that for a long time. My mind is fixed, my sight is fixed, fixed in my Beloved.

God bless you! I pray that God keeps you all safe. And he gives peace to each of you and peace for your country. Love your neighbour; treat them as you want to be treated, with respect and love. Remember the words of Jesus, 'And the Kingdom of Heaven is within you!' Speak the Truth and the Truth will set you free! You never know when God is going to come to you. He can come in any form, in any person. Watch your words, watch your thoughts, watch your actions.

God bless you! You may go quietly.

3.

Angels Are Amongst Us

STEPHEN: Good morning, everybody!

AUDIENCE: *Good morning!*

STEPHEN: I was in the graveyard today and I said 'Good morning to everybody!' there and I got more response than here. Maybe some of you are dead, but don't realize it. Good morning everybody!

AUDIENCE: *Good morning, Stephen!*

STEPHEN: You see! Is that so hard? What is the matter with people today? They put themselves in boxes, tiny little boxes. We call them houses. This is our territory. I am king. And we hold the voice of court. When we come out, where is our power? We have left it at home. It is all right being a king at home, but you should be king and queen in everyday life. You deserve it. Why do I say this? Because you have come a very long way. I don't mean coming here today, that's nothing. I am talking over billions of years, when evolving consciousness on the planet and before that when the Earth was forming.

Why did life not appear on Earth in all that time, why did it take three billion years? What is life? Life is consciousness. Without consciousness there is no life. You are conscious, aware people. To get to where you are today, that journey has been long and hard. And you may not even think about it. All you can think about is this life now. Some of you may think, 'Oh, it is such a long lifetime!' But speak to older people; as they get closer to the grave, they say, 'Oh, a lifetime is very short!' It's your point of view; it's where you are at this moment. If there is life, then natural law suggests there is death. If there is death, spiritual law says there is life. And this is why every great teacher, prophet, Master, has come to this Earth to give you exactly the same words: 'You are a creation of God, frozen in time and space.'

But what is frozen? The unit that you call body is frozen. This frozen unit actually is frozen light; light that has been condensed, has been changed into matter. So condensed that we can say it is frozen. And evolution is about unfreezing this unit, letting go, chilling out, thawing out, enlightening yourself, warming yourself up. Because when you understand the spiritual laws involved in the nature of man, it's about heat. When you are in passion you manifest heat. When you raise the energy from the kundalini, it is heat. So, you start to unfreeze, the unit becomes freer, lighter, more strength, more commitment – the eyes begin to lighten out, the thought system changes, and your material and spiritual life alters; it alters with your stage of consciousness; you are evolving. But evolving into what? What is the next stage? Where do we go from here?

Well, if you take the words of Jesus, 'Ye are Gods.' Think about that. 'Ye are Gods.' That is quite an explosion inside, when you sit and think about it. But what did he add to that? He added the fact that the kingdom of heaven is within you. Now, if you combine the two you can understand his reality. Because it is very difficult to bring your reality into somebody else's thought pattern, unless that person is a great Master and you give him permission to enter your reality.

When I work, you give me permission to enter your reality. So, when I enter your reality, I look at your whole life: past, present and future. I know your past, I know your present and I know your future. I know your karma, what you have done in your past life, why you are suffering in this life, and what grace God is going to give you in this life. Sometimes you are ready to accept the grace from God; this unit is unfrozen enough to take the divine energy of the Lord. Then the body lights up and present karma is cancelled out.

God always gives you something when you come to see me. Why?

Because, before you come to see me, your soul has cried out, 'Oh, God, help me!' And God has answered you, directed you to see me. In your lower, conscious mind you may think, 'I heard about this man. I will go to see what it is about.' But, do you think it's just coincidence that you have heard about me? You think it's coincidence that your little legs took you there to me? Of course not. There is a plan, a divine plan of God. Because you said to God – your soul said to God – 'God, help me!' And God says, 'Okay.' But you know, you have to be careful with that as well, because we don't always get the help that we think we want.

You see, God knows us better than we know ourselves. So God says, 'I will give you what you need, not what you want!' Look, I am a man. Like most of the men here, I like toys – toys for boys. It's true. We don't always need them, but we want them. I want this nice big car. I know, I can read your thoughts. You can hide nothing. I always try to explain it like this. Try to imagine you have a lover; a lover so perfect that this lover gives you everything you need. A lover that you can wake up at one or two o'clock in the morning and have a conversation with. Doesn't matter what it is about. That's the kind of lover we are talking about. Now, what happens if you wake your partner up at one or two o'clock in the morning? 'Wake up, I want to speak about my new car.' 'You are crazy, go back to sleep.' But, you see, my lover is there 24 hours a day, and I receive what I need.

Do I scream and shout like a little boy every now and again? Yes! Who wants to grow up? I am very happy to be a boy! I have two older sisters and they always called me the boy. It's true. I am the boy. And now I am over sixty years old and I am still a boy. Quite good. So, I like being a boy, there is nothing wrong with that.

Jesus said, 'as a child'. 'As a child.' Look at the innocence of children. I am not talking about those indoctrinated with war, but the basic innocence of children. They just love unconditionally, like you did one time. You were also children at one time. Maybe some of you haven't grown up yet, but we are all children at heart. But the world is coming at us, and from innocence creates a monster. So, evolution is about unblocking, about melting, about heating out.

Sometimes in your prayers you say, 'Oh, God, send me help!' And then you forget about it, but God doesn't forget about it. He knows if you really need that help; he will send it to you in the form of angels. Some of you will say, 'I don't really believe in angels.' But lots of you believe in the devil. Well, angels exist, let me tell you this. Not only have I spoken with them, but there have been photographs taken of me with angels.

Now, where do these angels come from? What are they? Remember, if you think about history, we can see that the prophets all had communications with angels. Moses, Abraham, Mohamed, Jesus, Mary . . . the list is endless. So, did all these people make it up? Why would they make it up; for what reason? Mohamed couldn't read or write, they say. When he went into a cave, it was angel Gabriel that spoke with him, and gave him the words of God. And when he came out of the cave, he physically met and saw Gabriel. And the stories about it are endless. And maybe one or two of you here have experienced the energy of an angel. I don't mean in your imagination, I mean actually in manifestation.

It was a year or two back when I was in Slovenia that the angel Gabriel took my body, and my clothes turned silver and golden pink and beams of light were coming out of my hands. These are facts. For me, it is a reality. It is a conscious reality, because I am experiencing it. Not only am I experiencing it, but the people there are experiencing it.

I will tell you a secret: when these things happen, I don't know who is more surprised, you or me. I never know what the Lord is going to do. I can tell you many strange stories. Where do these angels come from? Well we know they do not come from our imagination. So, let's go back to the creation of the universe, which has the shadow of ultimate reality. To understand that, we have to understand the words of Jesus. He said to us that there is a perfect world and an imperfect world! We are now, as human beings or units of condensed light or condensed carbon, living in the shadow of the perfect world. What does the perfect world look like? Perfect. Very similar to what you have in this world.

About one or two months ago, God showed me the perfect world. You may want to call it heaven, you can call it anything you want ... I could not put it into words for you. Lakes, mountains, but the colour ... there is no human colour to express it. It was pink – so beautiful pink – I have never seen anything like it in my physical life. Our world is a direct manifestation of the perfect world, but more condensed in vibration. When this imperfect world of ours eventually disappears, the perfect world will still exist.

What kind of body do you have in the perfect world? Well, to begin with, the one you have now, very similar. Can you imagine waking up in a perfect world? And, if there was a mirror and you looked at yourself, it didn't represent anything. Shape and form are still a necessity at the first stage of your perfect world. Then, as your consciousness evolves in the perfect world, so the body also drops away, becomes finer in vibration to match your conscious awareness.

So, what does that mean to us? It means the closer we are to God in our consciousness, the better the surroundings. That's to tell you in easy terms. On many occasions, I travelled to the perfect world and I came back here to this body. This body is not me. How can this body be me? Today it is here; it may not be here tomorrow. That which is, will overcome that which is not. I am not the body. I am that which is. Jesus told us that. I and the Father are one. And this is the truth.

The light we see by is manifested by the physical sun. But where do you think that light really comes from? It comes from the astral sun, from the perfect world. The astral sun will not burn out like the physical sun. But you see, man – while pure spirit – wanted to experience something greater than it was. Astrally, it couldn't understand what it was. In its consciousness it said, 'Is this all I am? Who am I?' So it had to create. And it created the imperfect world. We come to the story of Adam and Eve.

How did Adam and Eve come about? Spirit, because it was neither male nor female in its essence, had to create the opposite of itself. So it knew, by putting positive thought into one part of itself, it would create male, and negative thought into another part of itself, it would create female. So, from the one energy came two, male and female. Of course, it had to have a platform to experience from. So, condensed light was made into energy that made movement, made heat, condensed even more, and made matter that your body is now made of. And within each of us is this negative and positive flow of energy. As we know, when we first come to the womb of the mother, we are neither male nor female in body.

But there is a great planned work here. First a play of karma, of cause and effect – you cannot get away from it. You know, if you cut your finger it is going to bleed. If you catch the flu, it may take one or two or three days before it will come down. You can always see karma in action. So, we are born with karma straight away. So I suppose in some way you can say we are born in sin; sin of our past life. But, isn't it wonderful that we are given such an opportunity to live in this life, to experience this life and to evolve in this life?

Where do the angels come into all this? Well you see, from the dawning of consciousness God instructed the angels to watch over. You know they have many names and we all know the story of the fallen angel. But did it really happen? Well, symbolically the Fall of man did happen. Symbolically, Adam and Eve did happen. Now, if you think of the apple and you say, 'Well, surely it could not just be a picking of an apple from the tree and all this was created . . .!' Well, let's look at it in mystical terms. If you take a human, we look like a tree. Hair is the roots, the body is the trunk of the tree, the arms are the branches of the tree. If you turn me upside down and put me in the earth, the hair is the roots, the body is the trunk, the arms are the branches, but where is the apple? You see, *there* is the apple, the sex organ is the apple, that was picked in the Garden of Eden. That was when man fell from grace. He got so involved in the creation that he forgot the Creator.

The more we got involved in the playing, the more we forgot about who created it. It's like when you go to the pictures [movies]. You sit out there and you look at this big screen. Maybe you are watching a battle film. You know, there's explosions, people getting shot, blown up... And you are sitting there and you are so engrossed in the film that you think of all those poor people dying. But you see, if you follow the light of the film that goes right back to the projector, you don't look up there and say, 'Oh look, it's coming from there!' We don't even think about that. You are watching the film. And now you get involved in something, you know... maybe it is a love film, and you get so engrossed in it that it's you in that film. Now, when the film is ended, those in the big show that were blown up, buried, they get up and go home to their families. This is just a film. But you experienced it in your reality. It's the same in life. We got so caught up in this film that we forget what is behind it.

We actually say, 'They sing like angels.' We use this term, don't we? You know, 'There goes an angel.' But I tell you this: an angel can come up to you in the street, and you wouldn't know it. You wouldn't know that that is an angel. This happened to me on a few occasions. I am going to tell you one occasion of a great Master. He is in this world, but is about a thousand years old. Maybe some of you may have heard of him, he is Mahāvatār Bābājī. I was working in Denmark, and when I finished working I meant to go for a walk. And where I was working it wasn't such a safe place to go for a walk on your own. So they said to me, 'Stephen, when you go out, be careful!' So, I got dressed and I started walking along this narrow street, and the street was empty. And as I was walking, this man started to come towards me. Maybe he was fifty-years-old or so, and he had a beard and long hair and his clothes were dirty, and as he came closer to me I moved to one side so he could pass. He moved to one side, so I moved to the other side, and he moved to the other side, and as we kept coming together I kept moving and he kept moving, and I thought: this man is drunk. Remembering what was said, I had to be careful. I decided to turn around and walk the other way. So, I turned my back on this man that I thought was a tramp, and as I turned my back like this to go away, he shouted at me and he says, 'Bābājī!' And I was frozen in time. And I slowly turned around and he was gone.

You know, these great Masters, if they do not want to show you who they are, you won't know them. The same as angels. They can take on human form; they will look like you, they will speak, they will laugh and be sad like you. I experienced it more than once. Look, some of you know I have an ability — maybe I am in England — that I can materialize another body, maybe in Slovenia. I've been to some of your families and spoken to them, although I was in England. This is not magic, it's spirit. It's the force of my spirit.

Throughout history it has been written down. The Bible is full of these meetings with angels. Jesus even spoke to Lucifer. I don't think he liked him very much, but he spoke with him. Now, we haven't got to like him either, have we? Maybe we don't like the devil, but you would be very surprised how many people are influenced by Satan. And after your tea break, we will speak of Satan's influence on us and the battle that goes between the good and the bad angels, because you may think that all angels are good. Some are also fallen, and they don't want to go back to the perfect world. And the only way they can stop it happening is through you. While there is chaos on Earth, they will be there. And the fight between the good and the bad angels takes place.

You see, God uses us all in different ways. And you know, when you hear angels sing, it is not always the voice but what comes from your heart. You can have many good singers, but it doesn't come from their heart. And there is a difference. Difference is in energy. Because you know, energy is movement, it moves. You can take it, you can use it, you can enjoy it, you can love it or you can hate it. But you know, you hold the universe in your hand. Isn't that a strange thing to say as such?

You just do not realize your powers. Really, you don't. When you look in the mirror and you just see that face looking back at you, and you say, 'What power?' You have the universe inside of you! More than that – you have God inside of you. Hey, have you thought about that? [Silence, then mobile phone rings in audience.] God is calling us! You have God inside of you. All the Masters and prophets know this; this is why they spend some time of the day in meditation. Because meditation is the way we listen to God.

Prayer is the way we speak to God. And you know, sometimes you hear these prayers that are so long. I wonder what God is thinking, 'Oh, no, not you again!' Because I know that's what God was thinking about me one time. Because many years ago I wanted God, and I know God wanted me. But you know, you have to prove to God that you want him. Many people knock on the door, but the door is not opened for everybody. So I learned a very quick lesson: if you knock on the door, you have to knock louder than everybody else, and you have to do it constantly. So, eventually God opened the door, 'Stop knocking, I hear you!' You think I am not telling you the truth. That's true.

I shouted louder than anybody else. For many years my thoughts, my life, was God. 'God, I want you, I want you!' I didn't have any idea what God was. It could have been a cow flying in the sky. I didn't have any idea. All I knew inside of me was, I wanted God. I thought, well, I heard this thing called meditation, I am going to try to do this. So, I locked myself in my bedroom every single evening. One and a half hours I was sat in my room, just concentrating all my thoughts on God. And some years after that, in one of the meditations, God appeared to me. The light was so perfect that my body couldn't stop shaking. The heat poured from my body... This is truth that I'm telling you. If I stood next to somebody and I touched them, they would pull away and there would be burn marks on their body. If I stood here [next to a person], the person would start to sweat. Not me, the person next to me.

So, God answered me. But you know, I was never satisfied with little crumbs. I wanted all of it. Of course, God said, 'A little bit at a time.' It's like you have a donkey, you want a donkey to move, so you put a carrot in front of the donkey and the donkey moves. You see, I think God must have thought I was the donkey, because he kept giving me little pieces. And the more he gave me, the more I wanted. And I've been involved in this life quite a long time now. And I am still like a child; I still cannot get enough of my lover. But I know that to get more and more, I have to go inside.

I once said to God, 'God, what is truth? How will I find the truth and what is happening?' So, I went into a meditation, 'God, what is truth?' No answer. And I kept doing this meditation. And then one day the realization hit me: only in silence is there truth. Still the mind, still the breath, be still, it's that simple. It's that simple! *I am all there is, and there is nothing else. I am all alone. You do not know who I am till I created you. From myself I split myself to know myself. I am that I am.* It's that simple. It's so simple. Yet everyone wants to make it so hard.

People say, 'What kind of yoga should I do?' The great yogis predicted periods of Earth life; they split Earth life in four cycles: the previous cycle is called the *kali-yuga* age, which we started to come out of in the nineteenth century. That was the dark age, but still has an influence, like the oscillation of a fan. We are still trying to rise out of the influence of the *kali-yuga* age. And they say that the correct yoga for that age is *bhakti* yoga, but it is still paramount today. We still have to overcome our lower energies and tendencies through service and keeping our feet on the ground. *Bakhti* keeps a balance. Too many kriyas and overstimulation of the electromagnetism in the body can be dangerous when the foundations are not firm. Go slowly and get there safely.

What does *bhakti* yoga mean? It really means loving God. That your actions are Godly, that you think God, that you breathe God, that you act God; in other words: you live and sleep God. That's *bhakti* yoga. Throughout thousands of years you can see *bhakti* yoga in operation. One of the finest examples was St Francis of Assisi. Think about him, what he gave up and what he became. He was so in love with the Lord. Of course, as we go on there are many more. Many more.

We cannot all be Jesus and we cannot all be St Francis of Assisi or Mary. Everything in its own time, in its own place. There are many ways to get to God. You can walk, you can run, you get on a motorbike, even get a jet plane. My favourite song is, 'I'm leaving on a jet plane, don't know when I'll be back again!' Get a jet plane to go. Don't waste time. You cannot play at loving God. It doesn't work. You can fool yourself, you can fool your friends, but please, how are you going to lie to God? God knows you. How are you going to lie to God? All you are doing is wasting your time. And this is something you don't have a lot of in this world.

Look, your friend may borrow from you a hundred euros, and maybe if he is a good friend he will give it back to you. But where's the last ten seconds gone? You are not going to get it back, it's gone. That's another ten seconds closer to the grave. And if you have not had one thought about God in that ten seconds, you've wasted it. They are gone. Every time you take a breath, every time in your mind you say the name of God, you do something for yourself. The first thing you do is attract the divine magnetism and the electricity. This is how it's done.

As you are breathing, you are breathing something called *prana*. Now, if you could see *prana*, what it looks like is millions of little yellow dots moving around. Some of you have seen this. Especially on a nice clear day, when you are sitting outside in the sun and you just concentrate on the air, you can see all this *prana*. Well, every breath you take, you are sucking this in. These are electrically charged particles. They are like little time bombs, and when they enter the lungs they explode and the electricity is withdrawn from them. The electricity goes to 72,000 astral nerves. What is left comes out as carbon dioxide. But that electricity keeps your body alive. Now, when you add the name of God to doing that, it increases the electricity and magnetism. So, when you breathe this in, there is a sharp intake of energy. Of course, there is much more involved in it than I am telling you. People just don't understand how important your breath is and how we are governed by divine electricity and magnetism.

When Jesus said to us, 'Man does not live by bread alone', what did he mean? He didn't mean you need to have a pork chop! He was saying: 'Man does not live by bread alone, but by every word that comes from the mouth of God!' This is the whole sentence. So, let's take the last part of it: 'But by every word of God!' What does that mean to us? The word is *vibration*, vibration is the light. So, we cannot live without the light of God. Where is this light coming into us? Here is where it comes in [Stephen points to the upper end of the spine]. It's called the *bindu*. Light comes down and into here.

Without this light you do not live, you cannot exist. This particular light in this particular area is little known by people. When this is developed, when the yogi develops this area, and remember I am talking to you of something that is thousands of years old... You know, when you see the pictures of your saints they have a ring here [around the head], yes? We haven't the picture here, but there is a picture of me with this light manifesting at the back of my head. This is when the word of God is manifesting in such a high vibration that you reach into that state of awareness called cosmic consciousness. The word of God is with all of us, but not all of us realize it. That's the only difference between you and a saint. Remember the words of Jesus, 'Greater things than these shall ye do!' Who was he talking to? He was talking to us. He was telling us. It wasn't in the miracles of Jesus, it was in *his words* that the miracles were. They were the living truth; his words are living truth. And if you act upon them, if you truly understand them and put them into action, *ye are Gods*. You will come to my Father's house and I will make you a pillar and you will come out no more.[*] And these words were truth.

How can you go home if you don't know where home is? How can

---

[*] 'The one who is victorious I will make a pillar in the temple of my God.' (Rev. 3:12.)

you know truth if your whole life has been based on a lie? There is one great liar, and that was the fallen angel. Throughout the world it's called different names: Lucifer, Satan, Diablo. He has many names. And he commands an army so great, and the army is called legion. Don't think for one moment it doesn't exist. It does exist.

I've had firsthand experience of this. And all the great prophets have had the same experience. What does this evil look like? It can look like an innocent child; it can come in each and every form. So, you have to test the spirit. It cannot try to tell you truth, not for long. It will catch itself out as a liar. But you see, it is attracted by like-minded people. It speaks in your ear, especially when you are feeling depressed and you are trying to break out of your depression. He whispers in your ear: 'Listen, there is no God. God doesn't love you. Look at you, you are ugly. Who loves you?' We know, sometimes he is even more clever. He works on your ego: 'Jump off the cliff! If you are the Son of God, jump off the cliff. God will save you.' How many times have you been at the edge, if you would be honest with yourself? Of course, you don't want other people to know about it. How many times have you been at that edge, and you want to throw yourself off from it because you can't take any more pressure? What voice do we listen to? Where is it coming from?

Now, I know this evil exists. I've seen it, I've fought it. The last time was in Slovenia where I had to fight it in the cave of St Socerb. And the evil one appeared, and we got photos of it. We conquered him. Jesus appeared and Mother Mary appeared and witnesses filmed it. Wherever we go we have to destroy this evil, but we cannot destroy it with guns and bombs. We destroy it by truth, by love, by compassion. These are our weapons.

You must be thinking, well, how do I get to the point to do such things? Well, it's been a very long road from here. And I've had experiences and visions and physical attacks, manifested attacks. I was giving a talk like this in one auditorium like this in Bern in Switzerland. And it was actually more people than here. And as I started to talk, a wind started to blow around in the room — no windows were open – and you could feel this energy; and the wind grew stronger, and the evil, you could feel it. Of course, I had no fear of it. We could clear it. But the same thing happened in Israel, and it wasn't only wind that appeared; a dark cloud appeared in the room, and out of this dark cloud came a voice, the most horrendous voice you can ever imagine, and there were all these witnesses with us. And we had to fight it.

But you see this hand, this is the right hand of God. I've no fear of this, for I am not the body, I am the light of God. This is why every picture they take shows that my whole body turns into light. The same as when the light is coming from my mouth: 'Repent, or else I will come unto thee quickly, and will fight against them with the sword of my mouth.' This is Revelations 2:16. Everything that I do is in the Bible for you to read. For the God gives these prophets signs, symbols; he gives them the word, and the word is with God. And the word is, 'Let there be light!' Let there be light in your life. Turn your back on the evil of the world. Commit yourself now to the light of God. Say 'Yes!' to God. Say 'No!' to Satan. Say 'Yes, God!'

Because one day you will realize the truth. And if you don't start now, you are going to say to yourself: 'What a fool I have been, the Lord gave me the opportunity and I did not take it.' I am here to tell you again: The Lord is here with us to give you the opportunity. Take it with both hands. You don't have to make a long prayer to God, you need three words to say to him, 'Thank you, God!' If you would base your life on these three words, structure your mind on the [knowledge] that God is meeting your needs, you would be happy.

You say, 'But that's too simple!' The simple is the hardest. Because your monkey mind will chuck you everywhere. You will be sitting there, thinking, saying: 'Thank you, God, thank you, God... What am I going to do tomorrow?... Thank you, God! Thank you God... How much money do I have in the bank?... Thank you, God, thank you...' Why are we like that? Because of your lack of concentration. Unless you develop your concentration, you will do nothing in your life. Everything comes from concentration. If you want to sit and do yoga, meditation, you have to learn to concentrate. Otherwise it doesn't happen. You want to be a good lover? No, don't be a good lover, be a great lover! Whatever you do, put yourself into it, put your will into it, and you will also be marching towards God at greatest speed. Satan cannot afford to let you go. But you see, he is trying to influence you.

There is also another battle taking place, between the angels of light and the angels of darkness. In my last vision I was at the gates of hell, seeing this battle take place. There was so much energy being manifested there, that you could see this energy going from the gates of hell, overflowing on to the Earth. You could see it very clearly. That is this energy that the evil one uses.

I can try to explain what will be better for you. There is a saying that over battlefields the angel of death sometimes appears. Have you heard of this? Sometimes they physically see the angel up there. There are many records of this. This is when this evil energy takes on form. It will manifest as an angel. You see, its actions are different from the actions of the angels of light. And both can come in any form.

I am going to tell you another incident I had when I first started many years ago. I was sitting on the beach, looking at the sea, and I was saying to God, 'Where are you? I want you.' I had all these questions and I put my head down and I said, 'God, do you really hear me?' And all of a sudden I heard a voice. I shook myself and I saw a young man standing next to me. I thought, 'Where did he come from?' I thought probably he saw me sitting there... This young man, he had long hair, and the way he was dressed, I wasn't certain if he was a man or a woman, all I could remember was the very nice face. And we started to talk. He started to tell me what I was thinking. He said, 'God has not forgotten you!' And he started to tell me different stories. And the more stories he told me, the stronger I started to feel. It was like filling up the car with petrol. But it was his words that were filling me up. And he said to me, 'I have to go now.' Then I thanked him, and he started to walk away from me, and I looked up and said, 'Thank you, God!' I looked back at the boy, and he was gone. There was no way for him to go, he couldn't have gone anywhere. He couldn't have been any distance from me. I just said, 'Thank you, God!' and looked back, and he was gone.

These are the things I am telling you. These beings of God's creation are with us. Do you think God puts us here on our own? Do you believe that you walk alone? No. We only have to say, 'Please God, help us!' And instantly there is a reaction — maybe not always in the way you wanted, but instantly there is a reaction. And the battle still takes place between the good and the bad, even today. A lot of these people that are in power are very influenced by these evil energies. It's so difficult for them to speak the truth, because the truth cannot come from the great liar.

When I think of God I think of love, I think of happiness, I think of passion, of peace; I think of all the good qualities. But when I think of evil, I can't even say it, it sticks in the throat. Because you know in your hearts this isn't you. You know when you are very angry with somebody and you feel like you could throttle or punch them ... and after it's gone, you think: 'Oh, I shouldn't have said that! That's not me!' No, it's not you. The God within you is like a rose with beautiful petals and perfume. Make your life the rose that speaks silently in the language of love.

I was saying to you about at one time Gabriel came into my body and that all my white clothes changed colour. Now, Gabriel has been around ever since Creation and he is an extremely powerful angel. You know, very, very powerful. He's been around, wow — he's had his nose in everything, you could say. So, yes, they do walk with us. You must think: 'Well, how many angels are there if there are billions of people?' You've got to understand time and space are not their location. As I speak to you here, I could be speaking somewhere else. Time and space are not limitations. To you they are, because of your bodily vibrations. For angels they are not, and for Masters they are not. So, though I can be speaking to you here, I can be speaking to a group of people somewhere else at the same time. Because there is no time and space that governs the law of angels, or limitations.

You have the limitation of your body. How do you limit your mind? You can't. Your consciousness? Think of the moon, you are there. There is nothing quicker than thought. There is only one thing quicker than thought. It's non-thought. That is strange, isn't it? But beingness is a state of non-being: no thought, no light, no movement, just being. Until it decides to create, there is nothingness. And out of that nothingness comes everything. Seed is sown in the darkness of the Earth. As a symbol you can say that seed is creation. From the darkness of creation comes light.

You see, thought was first. Then came the word, then the light. You, my friends, are the light of God. You are the children of God. That's a fact. Some of you may not believe it, some of you may find it difficult to accept, but you are the children of God. And like all children, we will find our way home one day. How quickly, it's up to you. How much you wish to suffer, it's up to you. My advice: suffer little, but work hard. Get there quickly, but safely. There is much work to be done in this world and beyond.

You, too, can be workers of light. You all have the ability, you just have to develop it. Develop it in a conscious way through love, love, love. That's the way. As Jesus taught us: 'Love one another like I have loved you.' It's as simple as that. Why do we make it so difficult when it's so simple? Why do we have to hate when we could love? Why couldn't we share our food with people who are hungry, when we chuck it away in the trash can? These are all questions that have to be addressed.

But start with yourself first. Start to speak the truth to yourself. Start to live the truth. You are sentient beings in the body. You cannot die. Only the body will come and go. But you – you cannot die. But we are answerable for our actions. Right action – good consequence. Bad action – bad consequence. Truth – and live it!

Amen. May God be with you. And next time you want help, just call your angel. He will respond. I give you my word on that.

Jesus Christ was such a big lover of God. How long was his ministry? Three years. Yet it has lasted over two thousand years. They've tried to destroy it, remake it in all different ways, but they cannot get rid of the Truth. In the very words of our Lord, Jesus is the Truth, and that truth will set you free. I know that. You know why I know it? There are two reasons. First reason is that I don't believe Jesus was a liar. The second reason: I had my own experience of it. This is how we grow, through our experiences, and if we do not learn, we repeat the same experience.

And you know, not all experiences are good. You remember the First World War? That was a war to end all wars. Then, a few years later, the Second World War happened. And we still have to go through experiences of killing each other. Yet ninety-nine per cent of the population will say to the question 'What do you think of war?', that they hate it, because war brings misery, degradation, hunger, fear. This is what it brings. How can this be right to the children of God?

Jesus has never taught war. It was just love of our enemy. Love one another. Why do we make it so difficult? But if the truth is to be known, at some stage in your own life you have felt this anger inside of you. And with that hate, you make harm. But you see, we have to go on from this animal stage into man*kind*. Man is not *kind* at the moment. We have not reached that stage yet. We have to start to live the truth, to practice it in our daily life. Tell the truth to yourself. Don't try to change anyone else. Tell the truth to yourself and live it. And slowly, as you live the truth, you change. All of a sudden you have a smile on your face. The sunshine comes out of your eyes.

People say: 'What has happened to you? You are so different!' Then you can tell them your truth. And it's simple, isn't it? I'm in love. Start the day with love, fill the day with love, spend the day with love, end the day with love. That's the way to God ... and may God be with you.

4.

Aura Of Divinity

Let not one second be wasted. Let not the day pass away in vain. The most wonderful day is today. *God* morning to you. You know, we want a good morning, but it is better to have a God morning. What's the difference between good and God? One 'o'. We must take the 'o' out and become as nothing. How strange our lives become when we allow the attachments of our life to take us over.

Today we are to speak about the Aura of Divinity. In truth it speaks about itself. Most of you know what aura means and you also know what divinity means. Each of us possesses an aura. Some people's aura is more developed than others'. Why? Out of their spiritual realization. The great yogis of India developed their consciousness to a higher vibrational rate. We developed the vehicle of expression of that consciousness. It's like when you are buying cars. You can buy a very cheap car or you can buy a Rolls Royce. The quality is different. It's the same with you – the quality of your body, or I should say bodies, is different. Taking the higher vibrational energy and rise in magnetism evolves us.

When you look at the saints, there is a certain magnetism about them. Look at Jesus – I am sure some of you in your meditations have seen him. I have seen him … and his magnetism. His Aura of Divinity is so beautiful, so encompassing. How is it possible that one soul can evolve to such a degree of divinity? He tells us himself. By first accepting who we are. That's the most difficult part. It seems so easy, doesn't it? To accept who you are. But of course, you are going to say, well, you are the body. You are not the body! You are not the individuality or the personality. You are more than these things. These things come and go.

What is permanent? The spirit within you. As you intensify the awareness of your spirit within, by the law of attraction you draw to you these divine energies. Like now, as I am speaking to you, oil is coming from my feet and my hands. It is an automatic attraction of Divine Love. In other words, the more you give, the more God gives to you. It's that simple. It is not difficult. You don't have to have a degree in science, but it is better to have a degree in Love. To touch the very foundation of your being with this Love. And to face it. And to speak the Truth to yourself. And to say this is who I really am. I am not the outer shape. I am the fruit inside. I am the beauty inside.

When I look at you, you are beautiful. I am not looking at your bodies. I am looking at that what you really are: the Divine Essence, the Divine Values, the Aura of Divinity. This is what I look at. At this level, we communicate. At that level I am able to materialize another body to be at several places at once; to speak all languages, which happens. I don't bother to learn, it comes automatically, because when I create another body, I create it by the Aura of my Divinity. And the law of attraction of that divinity brings about all that is necessary. It may sound like science fiction to you, but some of you here know this is true because I have visited you in another body. It is not magic, it's your birth-right.

This is what Jesus came to tell us. First, he came to tell us that you cannot die. He proved it. Secondly, he said to us: 'Greater things than this shall you do.' Who was he talking to? He was speaking to us. Yes, you, me, you. It seems impossible, doesn't it? That we are able to do what Jesus did. And even greater than what he did. The answer is in the next words. In one of his discourses his words were: 'Ye are Gods!' If only you realize it! Now, of course, you say to yourself: 'We are Gods?' You look in the mirror, 'This isn't God looking back at me! I don't have any make-up on!' Or, 'I am not shaved!' But you see, you are only looking at the body.

Of course, we can go into the metaphysics of this and say, 'Yes, what Jesus said was absolutely correct.' Because if we think about it, what is the body? How is it created? It is created by matter. Atoms, electrons, neutrons, protons, photons, life-trons! Yes, but then we ask ourselves: 'How is matter created?' Matter is created by condensed energy. So how is energy created? By condensed light. So when we look at this principle, we see that light is condensed into energy, and energy is condensed into matter. So yes, your body is made up of light. That is the Truth. And if I say, 'How do we perceive God?', we perceive God as light. So, yes, we are Gods.

You see, God is not up there or down here. God is inside of you and you are inside of God. There is no separation. Absolutely impossible. But you exist as separate individuals and the Holy Spirit is within you. Now, the surprise is that there aren't seven billion different spirits. In truth there is only one Soul. And you gave that Soul a name. You called it God. It's the one Soul expressing itself through all of us. Wonderful, isn't it? And this is what every teacher has told us; that the Father and you are One. It couldn't be any different. But when you realize it, a metaphysical change *is* really incredible.

What's it about? It is about evolution. But evolution of life has no meaning unless it has consciousness. So life is a vehicle for the expression of consciousness, and it is your consciousness that is evolving – evolving from animal to human, through human to Gods. This was the meaning of Jesus's words.

Now, understand it is not just Jesus that manifested these holy powers. There are a few in the world who do the same thing, and have done the same thing through thousands of years. They are in touch with their real soul and that divine energy goes through them, as it can pull through you. You just have to develop it. How? You have to remember that people like Jesus and Moses and all the prophets were people like you and me. They had to start somewhere. So, lifetime by lifetime they developed their conscious awareness of divinity.

When you leave this life, you will spend some time in the astral world. Then you will come back. But what can you bring back with you? Only one thing: your good and bad karma. That's it. So the more good karma you create, the better the next life. You will be put in situations where you can develop more of your spiritual powers. Remember the law of attraction: like attracts like. It is not only on the physical level, but it is also on the spiritual plane. But when your consciousness is bathed in the light of the Beloved, you will attract that light to you constantly.

You know, we have hundreds of pictures when the light appears or flames come out of my hands or from my mouth. It is when you are in touch with that divinity that the outpouring of spirit would be manifested instantly. This is the power of will. Right thoughts, right actions. The action of drawing that magnetic force to you for development of the consciousness of your own divinity. People say to me: 'What prayers shall we say?' You can say anything. But for me there is only one prayer: 'God, thank you.' That's it. Because I am thanking God for the past, the present and the future.

When people come for the healing, I don't say, 'God, please heal them!' I say, 'Thank you, God.' So, in creating that thought, magnetizing that thought with my willpower, I attract the very essence of the Beloved. So, God says: 'Even before you ask, I have given it to you!' You understand that? That's because I go beyond faith. I go beyond belief. Knowing has become known. For me, there just is God. There is nothing else. Yes, we are the children of God, if you want to call it that. Jesus knew all about that. When he spoke, he spoke from the point of the Christ consciousness. He spoke from an authority. He spoke from the Aura of Divinity. And when people came close to him, his Aura of Divinity encompassed people and they were healed in body, in mind, in spirit.

When I am questioned, my answer is always, 'God is the doer of the action!' And that is the Truth. And by living that Truth, you set yourself free from the confines of your ego. And as the ego fails, the divine energy increases. Watch the ego! We all fall into the trap of it. I know. How can we stop falling into the trap of the ego? By watching, is one way. But the most important way that the Masters do, is to stop thinking. Of course, you cannot stop thinking one hundred per cent, but you can stop thinking ninety per cent. I taught this to scientists, so we know what this is about. The moment you stop thinking, you stop creating mental turbulences, because the mental turbulence is movement; it creates magnetism and this magnetism pushes out of you, pushing away that which you desire. So, desiring less is a much more positive situation for us. Still the mind, still the body vibrations, and see the true light that you are.

Some of you say: 'Will I ever see God?' Not in the terms you understand, no. In deep meditation, when you see the light, what you are seeing is your own soul. The light of your own soul. Jesus said to us that you have to withdraw from the Holy Ghost your bodily vibrations. In other words, you have to withdraw energy from the muscles, let that energy go into the Christ consciousness – through the Christ consciousness into the arms of the Beloved, uniting the Holy Ghost, the Christ consciousness with the Father. When this happens, you unite with the Truth. This is what Jesus was saying: 'To unite with the Truth.' From that Truth comes the ability to love unconditionally. For remember: love is an energy, like your physical love. Energy changes, but the Truth always remains the same.

We are sitting here, and I don't know all the people here, but we all have a different truth. But that is in collective reality. Of course, as your individuality, as your persona thinking and moving, using your imagination – and imagination is a wonderful thing – it is true that you can be Gods in your imagination, and the king of ego will be on the throne. That is okay. But it is not okay if there is no queen of spirituality. Behind every great man there is a great woman. You must have the king of materialism and the queen of spirituality. They must go hand in hand, nicely balanced. I say very simply: 'Feet on the ground, head in God!' It's that simple. Be in this world, enjoy it, but don't let the world be in you.

God never put you on this Earth to be miserable. You can have fun in the realization of God. God is not the God of vengeance, he is the God of Love. You have to understand it, because God's Love is much different from ours. God loves unconditionally. Human's love is conditional. So, how can we improve our energy? How can we develop this divine magnetism? How can we expand our energy field so that it also becomes the Aura of Divinity? But of course, it takes work. There are ways. Ways of meditation, there is a way through prayer, there are ways through yoga, such as *bhakti-yoga*, which is the Yoga of Love. There are different ways.

For me, in this lifetime it is the Yoga of Love. Just be in love with God. For me it is that simple. Just to be in love. Believe me, God knows if you have been true to Him. He knows. You can hide nothing from Him. He knows. But you have to give up things. One of the things you have to give up is a little bit of your time. To do what? To meditate. To go and speak to God. So many people say: 'Oh, I don't have time to meditate!' Well, get up earlier. Simple. You have time to read the papers, you have time to watch the television. Surely you can have a little time to sit and speak with God. But you don't, do you? It's always, tomorrow. 'I think I have some time tomorrow.'

It's strange how difficult it is to get into a good habit, and so easy to get into a bad habit. Meditation improves you, mentally and spiritually. Jesus and his disciples meditated through the night. And they used a prayer or a mantra. I can tell you one very similar to what they would have used. This is it: 'From the Christ's centre within me I call forth the Divine Energy of the living God!' It is an extremely powerful mantra. When you start to say it, you start to wake up the inner centres, you start to stimulate the Christ centre within you.

One of the centres that you will stimulate is the Bindi. This is the most important centre. As this gets stimulated, the next state is the Diamond. If you look at the Diamond, it's white with the tinge of blue. The most beautiful white diamonds have a blue tinge to them. I don't have it here, but we have photos when I manifest this energy of the Diamond, meaning: 'Die mind!' That the mind dies. How does it die? By stopping the action. And if there is no action, there is no reaction. Thus the purity of the manifested energy outpours itself.

It is the same with this: the light coming from the mouth. It is when the triangle, the Father, the Son and the Holy Ghost, is completely united, you are completely centred; and in that centre is a vortex of creative energy, or the energy of Truth. And that vortex outpours itself from the mouth. Now, in some books you may read about this, that the Masters do this. And in the Bible it speaks of it and says: 'Repent, or else I will come unto thee quickly, and will fight against them with the sword of my mouth.' This is Revelations 2:16. The sword of the mouth, the vortex of Divine Energy. I am able to bring this out and direct it towards evil to destroy him. This is the meaning of the sword. This is Michael.

As a matter of fact, when the next picture was taken, when some pictures were taken, Michael was above my head and you could see the wings. We have photos where you can see the wings of Michael. But when we bring this energy, we do not just bring the energy of Michael, but of Gabriel and many others. We have photos where Gabriel takes my body, where I am levitating off the ground, but the light of God comes into my head. These are things that are the creative principle of Divine Willpower. It brings about the change in you and others around you. This is by magnetizing the soul. The law of attraction comes into play.

So, I am forever magnetizing my soul with divine energies. How do we do it? We do it through saying certain mantras. I gave you one just now. It is very simple but very powerful. There are many other mantras… 'From the Christ's centre within me I call forth the Divine Energy of the living God!' These are extremely powerful words. As you say them, say them in your mind, don't say them aloud. There is more power in it when you say it only in your mind. Of course, there are other mantras that you would say aloud that are very powerful.

Now, how do we use the mantra? Well, first we will have to use it for forty days. You will have to do the mantra for forty days and you will have to say it one hundred and eight times. So, one hundred and eight times for forty days. This will magnetize your soul with that particular energy. But the Christ's one, you will use all the time. You will go within and you will meditate on it. If you do it correctly, you will be very surprised what will happen. What stops people is their laziness. That's what stops them.

Beautiful. You see, divine energy can manifest in different ways. One of the ways is through song. If you could see the vibrations in the ether around people when they are singing, you would understand exactly what I mean. Everything around us is in the sea of energy, all at different vibrations, light, grey, dark. These vibrations are affecting you. This is why God created the Holy Ghost, or if you want, you can call it Mother Nature. So that there is balance in the world, and it is in this balance that God placed his children. What is God's child? God's child is the consciousness. As a child, the consciousness evolves through millions of years. But what is millions of years in eternity? Nothing. And you will be surprised how many times you have done it.

You are older than time itself, and that is the truth. For we are out of time. I am not this body. This body is not me. Body comes and body goes. But I remain. I do not change. For I am all there is. But if I want to experience myself, then I come into the world of matter to experience that which I am not, to fulfil my perfection. I can only experience my soul through imperfection. But I do not forget who I am. From the sword of the word — energy of the word — of the expressed word.

You know, sometimes there's just nothing to say except to be. Just to find your centre. You see, most people say: 'Oh, we musn't be so self centred!' But this is not true. You must be self centred. You must centre the self, to establish the Truth. And within that centre, that manifested Truth is the vortex, the vortex so powerful that it creates universes. Ye are Gods! Would you believe you could create universes? I tell you: oh, yes you do and you can! Even now you are creating universes. You don't even realize you are doing it. How are you doing it? As you think, the thoughts are energy. The energy is positively or negatively charged. Because of the law of attraction, the negative will go to the negative and the positive will go to the positive. When you have so much of this energy, it becomes so big, so condensed, that vibration lowers, and that energy is then turned into matter. Ye are Gods! You are adding to the creation of universes just by the power of your thoughts.

Now, if you are doing this out of consciousness, think what you can do consciously! As you are coming to that realization of the self, when you establish the self in the centre of your being and you establish it consciously, uniting the principles of earth, fire, air, water and ether – when you combine these elements with your thoughts and your willpower, you can create anything, literally anything. So, you are made up of the same principles. All of creation is made up of these elements. But they are just elements. What brings them together? What is the kernel that holds them? What is the centre of fusion? What is the matrix that holds it?

It is the *gunas*.* There are three. From these *gunas* is established a centre of stability within, out of vibrational rings, creating five bodies. These five bodies are *koshas*.† And when they come down, they become more condensed. Of course, you have to go down before you come up. The last sheath on the coming up is the bliss or the causal body. This is the most difficult one to disengage with, to let go, because there is still a little bit of ego left. When this goes, your consciousness merges back with the sea. You don't lose your identity, but you have a wider field of seeing.

You are looking at me here, and your eyesight [vision] is limited. I am standing on the stage and my eyesight is more than yours. Just as if you are in a field. When you are looking into the distance, you can see a bit. But if there is a tree and you climb up the tree, you can see further still. So, in some ways you could say you are seeing into

---

* Qualities or attributes.
† Energetic sheaths.

the future. It's the same principle. After the bliss body, the past, the present and the future – you are conscious of it all.

A few times I have had this realization. And it is strange, because I could see out of the eyes of hundreds of people. What they were seeing, I could see. And on another way, when you are in that state of awareness you can even listen to the songs of the angels. Just after Christmas time, God showed me the Kingdom of Heaven. I can't put this into words for you. The beauty is beyond any earthly experience. And if you saw it, you would want to die immediately to go there. It is absolutely beautiful! Absolutely beautiful! And you know, the Kingdom of Heaven is just here, just hiding behind the veil.

Why doesn't God show it to everybody? Because he knows human nature. Everybody would want to go there before their time. It wouldn't be a Kingdom of Heaven any more. It would be a Kingdom of Craziness! You made a hell of this Heaven here; to die and make another one would be a mistake. You have a Kingdom of Heaven not only around you, but also inside of you. Would you know of this Kingdom of Heaven within you? Have you taken any time to explore it?

If you go on a holiday somewhere, you look at the holiday magazine, you read about it, or you get on to the internet and you look at it. But you do nothing about the holiday inside of you – the most magnificent holidays you can have. The Kingdom of Heaven is within you, and you don't have to take any clothes! Just your awareness. And that is so easy to pack. People cannot believe that there is this Kingdom inside of them. They read books, they may see some television programmes. But they are other people's experiences. They are not their experiences. And, you know, it doesn't matter what you read and what you listen to. There is nothing like your experience.

How can I tell you the beauty of the Kingdom of Heaven? I can say that the colours are not of this world. And what does that mean to you? You can imagine, you can wonder, in your imagination, something of a Heaven, but it cannot do justice as you actually see it. It's the same with love. Do you actually experience it? How can anyone tell you about it? If you have never had sugar in your tea or coffee, how do I tell you the taste of sugar? I can say it's white or it's brown, you put a spoon into water and stir it up, and it's sweet. But until you have tasted it, how do you know what I'm speaking about?

It's the same with spiritual realities. Until you are aware of inner values within you, you have only books and lectures that tell you of these things. Your experiences are the building blocks of your character. They mould and evolve your character, because if Jesus materialized in front of you now, it would possibly be such a revelation for you, that it would change your life forever. You would not be the same person that you were a minute ago. You would first start to question, did you see it? Did He really speak to me? Am I hallucinating? Was it true? These things come to your mind.

I remember when for the first time God physically spoke to me. I was in shock. And I heard His voice. His voice came about . . . I was sitting down in the meditation room, and as I sat down, I said: 'God, I love you so much!' And a voice came, very loud and very clear, and the voice said, 'My beloved son, I love you!' Over the years you start to question, 'Did I really hear it?' Oh, yes, I did! But I knew at the time that as time went on, I would question it. And maybe it's healthy to question, but it is also healthy to accept.

How many times has God got to tap you on the hand and say, 'Wake up!'? How many calls have you had and you did not listen to him? You pray to God and you hope He hears you. But of course He hears you; how can He not hear you? If He is omnipresent, how can He not hear you? He hears okay. He has good hearing. But He doesn't always respond; not in the way you want him to respond, because you always want something. 'Father, I want! I want!' What you want today, you don't want tomorrow. You keep changing your mind.

Well, you see, a Master doesn't change his mind. The Master is like an arrow, he shoots from the bow of the mind. The arrow is pointed at God. And let me tell you this: God is too big to miss. You cannot miss Him. But your arrow has to be straight. In other words, your willpower has to be strong to get you to that place of self-realization. For this is what it is about. There are no magic formulas. It's about vibrational rates that affect us, that affect our energy centres. These are affected by our thoughts. If you think correctly, your bodily vibration will change. The cells of your body have memories. Change the memory, bring about the light in your body. In other words, lighten up! Lighten yourselves!

By perfect harmony of your energy centres, you would have balance of your consciousness. It brings about a fundamental change in your whole being. For what is inside would manifest outside. In other words, that which is below will be that which is above, and that which is above will be that which is below. In other words: perfect harmony. You don't go anywhere, but you are centred: perfect centre of stability, not only physical, but cosmic vibrations of a Divine Nature that is centred in its Truth. This Truth will set you free.

Be still! Be still! In that stillness is perfect silence. There is only one sound: the sound of the voice of God. You may hear it as *Amen* or you may hear it as *Om*. These are the two sounds you might hear. What does the Om sound like? Where did you hear it before? Have you ever listened to a generator? Om is a cosmic generator. The word was with God, and the word was 'Let there be Light!' Ooooom … the generator starts up, generator creates heat, explosion, electricity, light and magnetism. As this goes outwardly, this becomes a day of Brahma, or the outbreath. This is cosmic evolution. Within this cosmic evolution is all of the creation.

Eventually, what goes out must come back. It may take a few trillion years, but once it comes back, the same thing happens again – out it goes again. You can't even imagine how many times you have been doing this. You think you are sitting here for the first time? No, this has been going on for eternity. You are eternal. And there's not just one of you, but in the *now* there is the past, now and the future. All happening at once.

Have you ever had a mirror in front of you and at the back of you, and you could see lots of you? You understand this? No? You know, when you look at two mirrors, you can see lots of you. In some way, you can say you are looking in the future and the past. For this is how the timeline is. For if God created the Alpha, he also created the Omega and that inbetween. So that which is here, is now there. Here and there has a movement. The movement is space. From space comes measurement. From measurement comes time. So, they are twins. Time and space are twins, they need each other. Why do they need each other? What is the purpose of their being? It is for us and our evolution, evolving from one thing to another, from the lower species to higher species.

What is evolving is our consciousness and the vehicles of expression. In ten thousand years, the body that you will be inhabiting will be much, much different; you may not even look like you, you may just look like bodies of light. Because as the consciousness evolves faster, the vehicle that it expresses itself through has to be that much more vibrant. So it is going to be changed. Certain organs will disappear. You won't need them. There will be a way of breathing that will give you food. Birth as you know it will not take place through a woman. Birth will be as it was in the beginning, when souls cloaked themselves in matter to rebirth themselves in the outer world, without coming through man or woman.

Angels can take on form just by cloaking themselves in vibrational matter. Nothing changes for them except location. Location, the only change. Their consciousness is the same, but location is different; from the Heavenly Kingdom into the earth kingdom. We've forgotten the art of doing it. Man sank into animal stage. Thus he forgot his true identity. He forgot that he is a divine being, and he encased himself into the body of flesh. Thus he became an animal. And he is still an animal.

You think your consciousness is evolving? In the previous *kali yuga* age, human consciousness came downwards, not upwards.

Most of you have not even gone past the second chakra. You still stand between the first and the second energy level. When you go in and through the second chakra, you'll reach the state of Shiva consciousness. And if you get one of these outside [holds up printed leaflet] you will see that fire appears in my hand and a cobra. Cobra is a representation of Shiva. This is because you go through the second stage or the second birth. This is why the triangle is not pointing up, it's pointing down. It's this way, so it's coming up from here, up like this and across here. In human birth this is the manifested state of your energy levels. So, as you go through the energy levels, the consciousness gets wider and wider. From this level down is body. From this level up is spirit. The fire is here [indicates heart]. This is where the little ember is, in your heart. You have to make this ember into a flame so it burns through the dross and creates the pure path. This is what Shiva does. He burns, he transforms, he cleanses, and he makes the path much clearer.

Every time you say 'God', you are doing something for yourselves, you are drawing to you the same energy. So, when you keep repeating the name, the energy is being created in you and around you, so that you are swimming in the sea of energy, but consciously.

Somebody is knocking at your door
Somebody is knocking at your door
Oh, sinner, why don't you answer?
Somebody is knocking at your door
Knocks like Jesus
Somebody is knocking at your door
Knocks like Jesus
Somebody is knocking at your door
Oh, sinner, why don't you answer?
Somebody is knocking at your door
Somebody is knocking at your door
Somebody is knocking at your door
Oh, sinner, why don't you answer?

Somebody is knocking at your door
Can't you hear Him?
Somebody is knocking at your door
Can't you hear Him?
Somebody is knocking at your door
Oh, sinner, why don't you answer?
Somebody is knocking at your door
Somebody is knocking at your door
Somebody is knocking at your door
Oh, sinner, why don't you answer?
Somebody is knocking at your door
Answer, Jesus!
Somebody is knocking at your door
Answer, Jesus!
Somebody is knocking at your door
Oh, sinner, why don't you answer?
Somebody is knocking at your door

Yes, somebody is knocking at your door. You have the key to open it. Why don't you do it? Why don't you take the key and open the door to your heart? Why don't you let God enter it? Let Him make his home in your heart. Let this little light become a flame in you. What more do you need than that? For there is hope in the knowledge that you and God are One. The hope is your evolving out of these conditions of your own small creation into the creation of Beauty, of Magnificence.

Many teachers are coming into the world today to say: 'Hurry up, change! Don't waste time because you don't have time to waste!' The world is in a mess. It's in a mess because of man's inhumanity to man. We cannot change the world, but we can change ourselves. When your neighbour sees you change, they see something different. People look at you and say: 'What has happened to you? You look so much happier! Something is different about you!' They may not even know what is different. But how do they know something is happening to you? Because of your Divine Magnetism. It touches people. It's like a hand.

And when you lay a hand on somebody like this, they move. They move. But you see, it is starting in unconscious ways. I say to people: 'Look, you can always tell if somebody fell truly in love. Just look at their eyes.' They burn with a passion of a thousand stars. The eyes tell you. Your eyes cannot lie. For they are the windows of the soul. And you know, if the windows at your home are not clean, you can not see out. The same is true with the windows of your soul. You need to clean them with the high consciousness. Allow that divine consciousness to run through you like water, cleansing and cleaning and balancing you.

It's a very simple act, to balance yourself. You don't have to go anywhere. You can do it in one minute. Done. It is simple to balance all your energy centres.

MEMBER OF AUDIENCE: *Will you explain how?*

STEPHEN: Come see me at the end and I'll explain how. You don't need to go anywhere for anyone to balance your centres, your chakras. You can do it yourself in one minute. Of course, with balance comes harmony and every centre or chakra is an instrument, you could say — one is a violin, one is a piano, one is drums, one is a harp; use your imagination. Before any orchestra begins to play, it sounds terrible, doesn't it? Drummers are drumming and some are blowing horns... But the moment the conductor comes, and the orchestra is brought to attention, and he starts, a beautiful melody comes, because the whole orchestra is in harmony. It is the same with your centres. If one of them is out of tune, all of them will be affected. So, they have to be in tune.

The 'I', which is the conductor, will bring about the harmony again by its knowledge of how to do it. Thus, the whole body, if you like, is a combination of harmonics — harmonics and light — and this is your nature. So, practice your meditation, fix the mind on the Beloved and you will see: the Beloved will be with you and speak to you.

Thank you for coming. I leave you with only one thought: Make your life a rose that speaks silently in the language of Love!

Oh happy day
Oh happy day
When Jesus washed
All my sins away
Oh happy day
He taught me how to watch
Watch and pray
And live rejoicing every day
Every day
Oh happy day.

<u>5</u>.

The Prophets

Who is Stephen Turoff? For sixty years I have asked the same question. Who am I? Am I really this personality that is known as Stephen? Am I this individuality that thinks, breathes, eats, speaks, sleeps, or am I something far greater than that? Have you asked yourself the same question? Do you believe that you are your given name? Do you believe that your life consists of eating and sleeping, being happy, being sad, being angry, being in fear? Is this your life; is this who you really are, or are you something far greater than that? Are you something that cannot be put in a body; are you something that cannot be the subject of words; are you something so vast that there is no beginning or there is no end?

What am I, my Lord, if I am not your child? The Lord gives us signs, but how many are blind to them? They ignore the signs of today. How many of them have ears, but they cannot hear the words of God, when these holy men come amongst us and tell us to repent? My hand will be upon you and still you don't listen. There will come a time when humanity is on its knees. 'Repent, or else I will come unto thee quickly, and will fight against them with the sword of my mouth!' This is Revelations 2:16, the word of God. Are you listening?

The prophets who are in the Kingdom of Heaven look down upon us and try so very hard to inspire us, away from the wickedness and the sin that we are living by. Yes, we are weak, we are made of flesh and blood, we have our emotions, but we are the child of the Beloved. If you see your child in trouble, what would you do? Tell me, what would you do? You have children, you speak nothing to them of morality, of human values; they know nothing of these things. And you say you are a good parent? If you cannot teach your children anything, because they do not listen to you any more... What about the children of Israel?

When Moses went upon the mountain top and he spoke with God, he came to bring the law, and Jesus came to soften it. Have you forgotten the Law of Moses? Have you forgotten the love of Jesus? How do you live your life daily, by bread alone, or by every word of God? You run quickly to God when you want something, and after that you forget him so quickly when everything is wonderful for you. Moses stayed upon that mountain while the Israelites were at the base of the mountain; they could not even wait for Moses to come down before they went back to their old ways, made idols of gold covered with the blood of animals, and fornicated.

God spoke to Moses, not just from the heart, but through the bush that burned, and by the finger that wrote the Commandments. 'This is the law I give to my people of Israel.' It was such a happening for Moses that his hair turned white and his spirit turned white; the cosmic energy was so intense that he could not look upon the flame of the Lord. I know this flame! For it appears with me. I don't just say that – people see it and film it. I know this flame! For it is the flame of Truth! It is the Lord's finger and it points at us. He came down that mountain with the Commandments in his arms. He was so pleased! Can you imagine it?

Not only did God speak to him, God gave him the Commandments, how the human race should live. And he came to the base and he heard the great noise, and they were making merry. On seeing this, Moses was so angry, he took the Commandments above his head: 'Oh, children of Israel, you do not deserve these words of God!' And he threw them down at them. You think that's all that happened? The ground opened, fire appeared, and many screamed, for they knew the mistake they had made, but it was too late for them. They sold their souls to the devil. They did not trust in the word of the Lord, but they trusted only in their ego, only in the gold and the riches. They paid their price.

Those that remained drew close to Moses; they picked up the Commandments, now in pieces. Moses went back up and prayed to God: 'Forgive them, for they know not what they do!' Do these words sound familiar to you? Think about our Lord upon the cross: 'Forgive them, Lord, for they know not what they do!' The Lord appeared and again his finger wrote, but this time God gave him instructions how to make an ark to carry these holy words. When he came down, they built the Ark of the Covenant and the Commandments were always carried in this Ark.

The only people who could carry this Ark were four in number. Why four in number?

North, east, south, west. For the Ark was so powerful, anybody coming within two metres of it would die. They would burn. Radiation from the scripture was so intense, that only those of a pure heart could carry it. God punished them; for forty years they wandered in the desert, and if truth be known, until today the Jewish race still wanders the world. The Lord has given them [the Commandments] to Moses; that was perfect for that time.

But Moses himself, he was a great soul. And God tested him, as he tests every one of us. But you see, Moses trusted the Lord. He trusted him. What do you trust in your life? What do you trust? I tell you what most of you trust. When you look at your bank balance – this is what you trust. One day your bank balance will be worthless and you will see you have wasted so much time. For since the day you were born, the Lord has been calling you, and you have not listened. But you see, the Lord does not give up on us. He is patient. He knows one day you will come back to him. But until that day you will suffer – you will suffer the pain, the fear, anger, hate; you will know what it is like to be alone, to be unloved, for all these are things of the ego, not the things of the spirit.

Forty years they wandered. And yes, they went to war, many wars. And God smiled upon them. And in every war they carried the

Ark of the Covenant. Even in Jericho, when they marched around Jericho for three days carrying the Ark ... then the trumpets were blown, and the walls of Jericho came trembling down. The prophets laid their lives down for us, to give us the truth. Every age the prophet has come, and every age you have crucified them, one way or another.

You think you can do without the prophets? Look at the mess of your countries. Look at the mess of the world. Because you think you can do without the prophets. You think you can do without the guidance of the Lord? You think, because you live in the twenty-first century, your intellect is so vast? And yet you don't even know the truth that Jesus said to us, 'And the truth will set you free!'

Though we always see Moses as an old man, he was also a young man, brought up in Egypt. And we know the story. How true is this? Most stories were told upon the desert winds; the desert abounds with stories of the prophets. Moses picked up a staff like this. You know the story of the staff? When he chucked it down in the presence of the king and it turned into a snake, and the Pharaoh's magicians got their staffs and threw them on the ground, they too turned into snakes. But what did this snake of Moses do? It attacked and destroyed the other three snakes and became supreme. Moses picked up the snake by the tail and shook it, and the staff was whole.

What is the symbology of this? It's the symbol of the meditator — those that walk the straight path, that's what it means. What is the straight path? What does the staff represent? It represents the spine. What did the snake represent? It represented the *kundalini*, the energy of the spine. When it ate the other three serpents, it conquered the three fundamentals of human nature: the three *gunas*. [Someone's mobile phone rings and Stephen says: 'God is calling!'] So, what does it tell you about Moses? It tells you that he was in contact with God through his daily meditation. He had the truth of the sages of ages, the same as Jesus, when he spoke of the straight path. If you follow me and walk the straight path, you will come into my Father's Kingdom and I will make you a pillar in my father's house and you will come out no more. Until you conquer your base nature, you are subject to the wheel of karma of life and death, of birth and death.

The prophets told us about this. They didn't just tell us, they lived it. They lived the straight path. But look what has happened! Man has conquered nothing. He thinks he has conquered space, making such strides in science, but he has not conquered his base nature. You think you are heading for the golden era. Go back further than the Bible to the writings of the *kali yuga* age, and it speaks of this period – of man's inhumanity to man, when the consciousness of man is not mastered but is going back into the animal nature. Even animals do not behave as some humans do.

You cannot turn your television on without seeing some violence; you cannot pick up some paper without some violence – without people making profit from other people's misery. Did you see yesterday in the paper, that three New York money men had a bet that the housing market would collapse in America, and they won two billion dollars? Souls are crying out and nobody listens. Children are crying out, mothers are crying out throughout the world. Who is listening? They give them food with one hand and they sell the guns to the government with the other. And they think you are so stupid that you don't know. Very cleverly they have disempowered you, and very cleverly you have given them your power! You have disempowered yourselves.

Everything the law of God rejects, you have accepted. So you pray to the golden idol? Soon the golden euro … the most corrupt organization in the world. Where is man's humanity? Where is it? You celebrate Christmas, but for what reason? Because two thousand years ago a child was born? What do you know of this child? What you were told. Have you had any direct experience of it? Have you gone within? Has the Lord Jesus spoken to you? Did the prophets come to you? Have you cursed out devils? You cannot even curse out the devil that is in you, let alone curse out the devils from somebody else.

The devil has your ears. When are you going to say 'no' to him? When you are going to say 'yes' to God? When are you going to take up the staff of your own life and march and say: 'Enough. I am a child of God and all these are my brothers and sisters.' When you go on a battlefield, and the battlefield has been cleaned of bodies, and you see pools of blood, what colour is it? Tell me, you only see a pool of blood. Is it of a Muslim? Is it a Christian? Is it a Jew? Is it a man? Is it a woman? Is it a dog? What is it? How can you tell? It is the same blood that runs through your veins. It is the same blood that Jesus gave on the cross. Jesus did not live in self-denial, but you do.

You turn the television off. You look at the paper and put it away and you say: 'There is nothing I can do!' This is how we have become a nation of slaves! One way or another, we are slaves. And you think you are free? You fight wars for freedom, and there is no freedom. There is no freedom in war. There is no freedom in hate. There is no freedom in fear. The only true freedom is the freedom Jesus told us: And the Truth will set us free.

'Amen!' said the Lord. For I am the 'Amen'. I am that I am. I am all there is and there is nothing else. I sent my prophets upon the Earth to you to tell you of things you do not yet know. You put their words into books but you've lost the Truth. You look at the words, but you do not understand the meaning. When you tell yourself one lie you have to tell yourself another and another and another ... until you don't even know what is a lie and what is the truth. This is the same with all human beings. Yes: 'Only the Truth can set you free!' But what is that Truth?

Even in this little hall, each one of you have your own truth. Now, think of this as a world of six billion people, all with their own truth. So, what is true? This is your collective reality. Be in it if you want to be, playing the game of life. Sometimes you enjoy it, sometimes it gives you great pain. But like all games, games have rules. God laid down rules to this game of life and you ignore them. You ignore the prophets. You do not live by the law of God anymore. You live only by the law of man, as your culture, your collective reality, gains strength. So you make more laws, until you are lost in your laws. Your laws do not bring you peace. Look around you! Wake up! Smell the coffee.

People still kill each other for no reason, and it's all about power. And that power only lasts while you live on this planet. You think you can take that power to heaven with you? If you think that, you will be in for a very big shock. If you think that because you are a president of a country, that St Peter will meet you at the gates and say: 'Come in, Mr President, we have a special place for you.' You think that? Jesus spoke of this. You can have a head made of gold, a body made of silver, legs made of platinum, but the ankles and the feet made of mud. Smash the ankles, smash the feet, they will be as nothing, the body will fall, it will be worthless. Only the Truth will get you into the Kingdom of Heaven.

So what is this Truth? What is this Truth that has been told for thousands of years and that has been told again now? That there is only one God and this God is within you and all around you. The Kingdom of Heaven is within and all around. Lift the stone, you will find me. Cleave the wood, I am there. I am there. When did you take time to look? You have such a busy day. Get up, make your breakfast, go to work, come home, cook your meal, look at the television, go to bed... And in all this time, what have you seen? What have you heard? The routine has become so monotonous, so insignificant that you do it like an automation. You go to work to put bread on the table, to give you strength, to go to work to earn money, to buy food, to give you the strength, to go to work, to earn money to buy food, to give you strength, to go to work, to earn money to buy food, to give you strength, to go to work, to earn money to buy food...

And we go on, and we go on, and we go on... Yet we forget who created the bread for us; we forget who gave us the breath in our body; we forget the ground we walk upon; we forget the sunshine upon our face; we forget the wind that blows through our hair; we forget the birds of the sky who do not sow, who do not reap, because the heavenly father feeds them. They have no fear. They fly high in the sky for they know they are safe in the arms of the beloved. But where do you fly? Into the arms of hell, and the hell I am talking about is here in your head.

Love, what do you know of love? What do you know of it? You look at someone or something and say, 'I love you!' And then next moment you put demands on that one you love. 'I love you, but...' From love comes conditions. From your great love for somebody you've started to condition it, and the moment you put conditions on love, it is not love, it's *demonic*. Because that love will destroy you or the person you aim it at. To love is to love unconditionally, to love from the heart, where God resides. God does not reside on your lips. Listen to the words that come out of politician's mouths. They smile at you as they cut your throat. The true words are unspoken, the true words come from the heart into action. Into *action*.

Let your life be *bhakti*, let your life glorify the name of God in your action, for your actions speak louder than any words. When you leave this life, let your family and friends say: 'There goes a good soul!' When you are going home to the Beloved, don't leave a bad legacy, don't let the people you know say: 'Thank God this witch is gone!' It's never too late. The heavenly father calls to you. It's never too late to turn your face away from the darkness into the light of truth, until that truth lives through you as it did through the many great souls and saints: Moses, Elias, Jesus ... many more throughout the centuries, throughout the world. They come for one purpose: to represent the right hand of God.

I had many visions and my visions got stronger. I met Jesus and the divine Bābājī standing together, and I knew that they were the right hand of God. They did not have to tell me, I knew. Jesus did not speak to me, but Bābājī spoke to me. I've come to bring you the

Word and the Word is with God. And the Word is God. It vibrates within your very being. I am the One God. I am the Law. Live by the Law. For if you do not live by the Law you will die by it. This is the promise of our Lord in the End of Days. Don't think it isn't here; you don't have to have any degree to read, you don't have to have some intellectual look around to see what man is doing to the Kingdom of God upon Earth.

Are you a part of this? I tell you this: you are much to blame, for you stand by and you do nothing. You watch but it doesn't affect you. So why should you care? You may shed one or two tears. Why do you care if a baby is dying in Africa or in Bosnia or Serbia? It's just another child; it's just another voice ... I am a voice in the wilderness crying out to you: Listen! Listen! Listen to your conscience! What is the heaviest thing in your being you can carry? You cannot carry anything heavier than your conscience. Be of good conscience. This is the true way – that your consciousness and truth be as the staff; let it be straight, firm and with commitment. In other words, let your spine be strong, that the love from your heart pour out, that the words from your lips be one of hope and comfort. Take your enemies into your arms and love them. Love them as Jesus told us: 'Love one another as I have loved you.' This is my legacy. Love them as Jesus told us: 'Love one another as I have loved you.'

John came before Jesus to clear the path. Who was this crazy man who came out of the wilderness, shouting and screaming louder than me? What did he live on? Honey and fruits of the trees, this is all he lived on. Some say he was crazy, others that he was a saint. Some wanted to be baptized by him, because in those days there was only one sect that actually baptized, and that was the Essenes. So it looks as though John belonged to this group. It was said they wrote the Dead Sea Scrolls.

John had wild eyes – they were fire. His body burned with fire. His heart burned with fire. His words burned into your very soul.

Why? Because he spoke the Truth. 'I am not the Messiah', he says. 'I have come to clear the path for the Messiah to come.' Jesus did not really start his ministry until he was baptized by John. When John saw him, he recognized him immediately, not from that life, but also from his past life. For in the last life the roles were changed. John was the Master of Jesus. God sent them back because man's inhumanity to man was so strong that man had to be saved from himself. The power of karma grew so black that men were heading for an abyss. So the plan was made in heaven that the Son of Man would come.

He never said he was a Son of God, even thou he knew it. The only one who truly knew it were the devils. Yes, this is true. For when Jesus went to cast the devil out, the devil said: 'We must go, the Son of God is here!' Jesus did not want people to hear this. 'I am the Son of Man!' – even though he had divine incarnation and he was a beloved Son of God, the same as we all are.

So John went to kneel before Jesus and Jesus stopped him and said: 'No John, by our law you must baptize me!' And as John stood there blessing the Lord, the Angel of God in the shape of a dove came upon the head of Jesus. You know this is the Holy Ghost. Of course, Jesus did not need to be blessed like this, because he said to John: 'John, you baptize by water, but I have come to baptize by spirit.' That is the power of a true Master, to baptize you by spirit. Jesus knew the road in front of him was long and hard.

When Jesus was in the womb of his mother, he spoke tele-pathically to her. Even when he was born, he could speak to her as he spoke to John, telepathically. For there is no time and space between great souls, for they are one with the heavenly father. There is no time or space; it does not exist. Yes, Jesus was born. It was no crime in those days to be born somewhere in a cave, in a house, in a stable. He was born, and nothing could stop it. Nothing could stop Jesus' march towards the Truth.

When King Herod heard of the birth, he commanded all new-born children should be put to the sword. But Mary, Joseph and

Jesus got away. They went into Egypt. Divine miracles were happening around the baby Jesus. The sick were healed just by touching. Miracles happened. Then they came out of Egypt to where Jesus grew up as a boy to the age of twelve-years-old. Why did he run away from home? Because he knew it was not his duty to marry. His father missed him, because can you imagine having a child with divine powers? His father was a carpenter, and many times a piece of wood didn't fit, it was too short. He would say: 'Please, touch the wood, make it longer!' Of course he did these things. He loved his parents, but he knew they were only biological parents. He had the divine Father and Mother that followed him from lifetime to lifetime. His divine Father protected him like his eyelids protected his eyes.

So he took a caravan into India, went to the Himalayas and stayed in a monastery – there is enough evidence for that. He studied there in various other places, while he connected his consciousness with the Christ's consciousness. When he reached the stage of 'I and the father are one!', that was the time his ministry started. Around about 26, 28 he started his ministry in India, Persia, Iran – he was welcomed in many places until he came home.

The Messiah – the chosen one. The Rabbis did not know what to make of it. 'Who is this Jesus of Nazareth that heals the sick and raises the dead? Is he a magician? The devil uses magic. Who is this one who says he is the Son of Man? He teaches the Law? He knows a lot about the Law implicitly, even in little things. How does he know such things? He talks well. Who is he?' First they had a little fear of him, then they loved him. People loved him.

Remember one Sunday when he sat upon a donkey and rode into Jerusalem, and they put palm leaves down? Can you see it in your mind? People were so happy and they were cheering and crying: 'Lord, you are here! Praise be to God, you are here!' Yes, 'Praise be to God', he says, '. . . for you will not have me for long. You have two tongues, as a serpent.' Then their love turned to fear. The fear turned to anger. The anger turned to hate: 'This is not the Son of

God, only the son of men, some mischief maker! Liar!' Can you imagine this in your mind? Put yourself there. Listen to it. First they loved him, then they feared him, then they hated him, then they crucified him. And guess what? They loved him again.

For two thousand years, Jesus is still being crucified. And you are letting it happen. How sad is that! A crowd is still longing for his blood. How sad is that! Maybe you are one of the screaming crowd? His mother looked on for she knew his time has passed, for he told her. And Gabriel appeared to her and said: 'Your beloved son is in our hands. Do not fear, mother.' Yes, he went to the Cross. Yes, he had a human body with divine powers. Yes, he suffered the pain on the Cross. But thank you, God, it lasted only six hours and it was done. Do not celebrate Christmas for the death or the birth of Jesus, but the opportunity that Jesus gave you. Celebrate the true birth of your spirituality.

We have bread and we have wine because the Lord Jesus, at the Last Supper, took this bread and said: 'Eat it, remember me, for this is my body.' Of course, we know a loaf of bread is not his body; he was talking about that which was created. 'Drink this wine in remembrance of me, for this is my blood.' It is the blood of the Earth. Water that the grapes drink is the blood of the Earth. 'This is my blood.' Do you see? Do you understand? So today we will share this together. We are going to bless the bread and the wine and we want you to take part in it, not thinking of the death of Jesus, but the birth of life. Let it be a new birth for you in your consciousness, in your heart, and let Jesus smile upon you as I know he will.

In the name of the Father, the Son and the Holy Ghost. In the name of the living God. [Stephen blesses the bread and the wine.] From the Christ's centre in me I call forth the divine energy of the living God. In the name of the Father, the Son and the Holy Ghost! Come.

We have come to that time when we have to say goodbye to each other. But we know there is no goodbye. You can never say goodbye to yourself, for I am in you and you are in me. God put you in this great country called Slovenia — S-love-nia — it's the only country with love in its name! Do not ask what your country can do for you, ask what you can do for your country. Be a shining beacon, let God shine through your eyes. Let his words fall upon your lips. Live your life with God and the prophets. Come back to the Lord. Come back to his Commandments.

You know the story of the son that was lost to the father, the prodigal son? And when he came back, his father was so happy he called for the sacrifice of the fatted cow. But the brothers were so angry; they could not see what his father saw. 'My son was lost to me, but now he is home!' You have been lost to the Father. I am the Shepherd. Come home, come home, come home.

<u>6.</u>

Let There Be Light

I have just been told I am supposed to speak, but *everything is within the silence*. So, let's start right. Stand up and turn to the person next to you. Put them into your arms and welcome them, 'Good morning, Beloved Self.' Get to know each other. What makes you different: body, personality, your individuality or your conscious awareness? Be aware consciously of who you are. Now you can sit, relax.

Hate comes and goes, leaving devastation. Love comes and grows into something very beautiful. People say, 'Are you going to give me knowledge?' Knowledge without wisdom is dangerous. Pick up a few books, you have knowledge, but it does not give you wisdom. Wisdom comes from your experience, your knowledge into action. And it's from that manifested action that comes the feeling, understanding of the Self.

I said to you once before, many of you, that there are only three questions you need to ask: Who am I? Where do I come from? And: Where am I going? And when you truly have the answers to these, there are no other questions, because there *are* no answers. Questions and answers are only in the field of conscious relativity. Another question leads to another answer, another answer leads to another question, and so on . . . In other words, it feeds your duality. And this is where we get stuck.

But I want to share some wonderful experiences with you that have happened to me very recently. You know, I have been very honoured over the years that God speaks to me; that when He speaks, His Light appears and people come to film it happening. But ten weeks ago we had something very special. I was working in the surgery in England and there was a patient on the bed, and we had a big white towel on the patient, and as I was working I was aware of the whole room changing colour. The patient opened her eyes and she saw strange energies in the room. I noticed the room turning pink, so I went outside and asked one of the helpers to come in and said to her, 'What can you see?' She said, 'Everything is turning pink!' I said, 'Yes!' Everything, the air ... everything was just turning pink ... My clothes ...

Then, the form of the Divine Mother appeared. We were so in shock. I cannot explain the beauty of her. She had those most beautiful large round eyes; they look like pools of water. She shone with an effulgence that is not of this world. She smiled at me and just said, 'Stephen, I am always with you!' She looked at the patient and she put her hand on the towel, and her hand was much bigger than mine, and when she took her hand off the towel, she left her handprint on the towel in beautiful pink. We still have this towel in our surgery in England. It's fading a little bit now, and when I put my hand against it, the hand is so big and the energy is so beautiful.

Why did she come? What attracts her to come? Love attracts. Live Love! You are Love! People say, 'I want to train to be a healer.' You don't have to go anywhere, there is nothing to train, there is nothing to do. There are only two things you need: the first is Love, the second is Compassion. Love and Compassion. These are the two things you need. Who can teach you to heal when you are not the doer of action? What is saying, 'I want to be a healer'? The ego is saying, 'I want! Look at me!' But in this duality you have to work within this field that's recognizing a force within as well as without.

If I was to stand here and I say: 'There is only God and nothing else exists!', what would that mean to you? How would you accept it? We use every excuse: 'I am the child of God, I am a part of God, I am a cell of God, I am the Light of God ...' You see, we use every-thing except the Truth. And Jesus said, 'Speak the Truth and the Truth will set you free!' Start speaking the Truth to yourself, don't try to tell the Truth to other people. The Truth starts with yourself. Otherwise you get caught up in mind games.

What is this mind game? Well, to understand this you have to go back to the beginning, when you were the Soul, before you took on this body. The Soul was free, it was the Master, it knew everything, it had no fear, it didn't even have Love; it was beingness beyond the understanding of Love. You see, we talk of Love, but what do we know of it? We speak of it so freely, 'I love you!', 'I hate you!', 'I fear you!', 'I am in comfort with you!'. We use these simple words to express a feeling. What feeling? What is your feeling now? Where are you in this moment? What is your feeling?

As this spontaneous feeling warms up inside of you, you react to it. It's an action, or it's a reaction of the action. This is exactly what Jesus said, 'Turn the other cheek!' What did He mean? He meant: don't attach to the action, then there will be no reaction. Stop it! Stop the force behind the action. Then slowly, as you practice this, the karmic implications slow down. So, you see, the Soul is free. No pain, just bliss. Then it decided to take the body. And, you know, the moment it took a body, it took on two slaves: the first slave was the mind, the second slave was the body itself. And the Soul was the Master. But look at you, you don't look like Masters to me. Why is that? Why? Sit quietly for a couple of minutes and ask yourself that question. Why are you not the Master?

Close your eyes, ask yourself the question, 'Why am I not conscious of being the Master?' You are not conscious of being the Master for one reason: you disempowered yourself and you gave your power to your mind; then the mind is the Master and you are the slave. And you run behind the body like a dog. And the mind is so clever; it chucks you scraps of food from the table of life. And you are so happy with it. Oh, of course, you complain from time to time, but you don't do anything about it. Why do you do nothing about it? Because when you give your power to the mind you disempower yourself. You are powerless to act in the Light of God.

So, what is the Light of God? The Truth. Jesus said, 'Live the

Truth and the Truth will set you free!' Free from Satan. What did He mean when He said, 'Satan, get behind me!'? He was talking about His ego, because it blocked Him from the Light of God. We all have our Satans. We all have our monkey minds. Your power is given to the mind. Now you have to take it back. Why should you be happy with only the scraps from the table, when you can have the whole feast? When you could be sitting at the head of the table and enjoying everything?

You think you came here to suffer? Not true. Would you put your children into a school knowing they are going to suffer day after day? You think God would do the same thing with His children? Not true. He gave us a wonderful thing, it's called free will. You see, God's will is my will, but my will is not God's will. If I were to do God's will, the whole game would be finished, because I would in fact be doing my own will. In other words, I would be fully aware of who I am.

You use all these mantras, for what? Only one thing sets you free: Love sets you free. Love – Love – Love – sets you free. What is the mark of a true human being? Of course it's Love – Love – Love. We are only growing into human beings, we are not quite human yet. So, how do we take back our power? By stopping denying ourselves. To stop denying the Self. The Self is all powerful. If you allow the Self to take control, you will be absolutely shocked by your capability.

I called this seminar 'Let There Be Light', but what else does it need to be called when it is only the Truth? You truly are the Light. When you live it, think it, eat it, sleep it, you become it. There is nothing else but God. Tell me one place where He does not exist? There is no place. God is within you and you are within God. So, what does it tell you? What is the first surprise? That you have never been separate from God. God is not in Heaven while you are on Earth. There is nowhere to go. There is nothing to do except to be your-Self. The Self is Love. The Self is unconditional. The Self asks nothing, only the ego asks. So we need to take our power back. We need to say yes to our-Self. To listen, and this is the Present.

What is this Present? Let's think about it. Every night you die, you go to sleep. Hopefully you wake up. So every night we die to this world. And every morning we awake to a new birthday. Every day is your birthday from your miniature death. And on your birthday, people give you gifts. So what gift do you think God has given you today? Today and every day God gives you the Present. This is His gift to you. The ever Present. So, what is the gift of the Present? It is so simple; you have to be blind not to see it. This is the Present of God [points at the empty piece of paper on the board]. Where is this blank sheet of paper? Where is this drawing board? It is here, in the mind, ready for us to put beautiful things on; or, if you want, ugly things. But remember, what you put into this is only a reflection of the self. The lower self, not the higher Self.

Higher Self. Lower self. This blank board is there for you to write on. We are creating the picture of our daily life, of how we want it to turn out. Everything on this picture causes positive and negative vibrations. They manifest within as well as out. This manifestation is in you now. That very essence is within you; you have created it since you have awoken. Now, because they are in movement, it creates vibration and magnetism. This magnetism emanates from you, and people are attracted or pull away from you.

When you look at somebody that is in the Love of God, you are attracted to them. Why is that? Because of their magnetism. They are in touch with the higher Self. So, they are able to magnetize themselves. And it is this magnetism that has certain qualities. Of course, you have physical magnetism, but I am talking of divine magnetism. Look, as I speak to you now, oil is coming from my hands. It is sticky. What is this? This is divine magnetism. What is divine magnetism? It's keeping the mind on the higher Self, not the lower self.

I said to the Divine Mother this morning, 'Divine Mother, what are we going to do?' She said, 'My son, I will be there!' So, maybe she will transfigure me or Jesus may transfigure me. I don't know. But transfiguring of what? It's not so much transfiguring; it's blending –

blending of energies of magnetisms, of electricities, of Light. You see, Light will blend with Light. This body cannot blend with this body, but her Light can blend with my Light. You can become One with the Light.

Now, I am going to tell you the Truth. There is no One with the Light, there is no blending with the Light, you are the Light. You cannot blend with yourself, you only think you can. This is another game of the mind. You see, it's the mind's job to keep you away from finishing the game, to the realization of the Self. That's why you created it. But of course, you can't believe that at this level. You are not accepting it. You say, 'I would not put myself in such a mess!' But you have. Who gave you the mess? It was the Present that has been created by your lower consciousness. All you have done is to give away your power and now it is wrong to take it back?

Why is it you can love everybody or most people, but you cannot love yourself? Why do you have to make other people love you, so that you can feel loved? And if these people don't love you, you feel sad. It's a part of the game of the mind. You see, you go up and down, up and down… Love and fear, love and fear… This is the spectrum on which most human being exist and base their happiness on. Of course, it is more complicated than that, but if you take all the complications away, these are the two places you live. If you are in love, you are in fear of losing it, and it is strange when things are going so good for you. You say to yourself, 'Why is it going so good for me?' That is so alien, it should not happen for you. Better still to hit yourself in the face, then you feel better about yourself. Then you feel quite good. You might be miserable and sad, but you know feeling good was only a little fluke.

How can I be in love? You know, if I am in love it could be taken from me. Maybe I should love this person, hoping he will love me back. Do you think I care if he loves me or not? I love him. I love you all. I love you unconditionally. I don't care. I love you just for the sake of loving. But people say, 'Surely you cannot love people who kill and hate!' Where would be my philosophy if I only loved the people that love me? I have to love everybody, because when I look at everybody, I only see God. Now, I love the God within you. I may not love your actions, because your action does not serve society in a positive way. So, society grows as a whole, and what are you doing?

What are you doing with your lives? This physical life is so short. It is but the blink of an eye in eternity. You know how lucky you are to be in love, to touch each other, to feel each other, to love each other? This is how you are created – the passion within you, so that you want to join together to become One. This is the very height of your passion, when you say 'yes' to yourself. When you are in the height of your passion, you scream: 'Yes, God!' It is a feeling; it is a sensation of your body, of your mind. Everything just goes from you and you feel one with that Energy. You are that Energy. It is not separate from you. I have come to tell you this. I have come to show you the Light. I am only a reflection of you. Whatever you see in me is in yourself.

Can you not feel it? Can you not feel the Sea that you are in? Just reach out for it; you are in the Sea of God now. You are not separate from it. Feel it, let it enter you; the only entering is in your consciousness, the awareness. Stop punishing yourself, come into the Light. We are being blessed with the Divine Light now appearing. The beams of Light are coming down. Close your eyes, just breathe in that Light. You will feel your body getting hot, your hands will start to tingle.

We are so honoured here, the angels of God are walking amongst us and the Divine Mother's Energy is here. Just smell the air; you can smell it. The Power of Love can set you free. If you close your heart, what can enter it? It's time to say yes to yourself. It's time to say 'Yes, God!' 'Yes, God!' I want you to start breathing through the mouth. Open your mouth, and as you breathe in, I want you to say, 'Yes!' And as you breathe out, I want you to say, 'God!' 'Yes, God!' The angels of God are with us. Speak with God. Take two minutes to speak with God. God is speaking to you, and you are answering

Him, 'Yes, God!' As you are doing this, the angels are working with you.

Can't you hear them? They are affecting everything. They are affecting all the sound. Reach out to your angel, reach out to God. 'Yes, God!' 'Yes, God!' 'Yes, God!' 'Yes, God!' Reach out, let the ego go! Reach out, 'Yes, God!' 'Yes, God!' Reach out, God is waiting for you. God is saying yes to you. You cannot say yes to God? Is it so hard? Is your ego so big? What you are doing is setting yourself free now. Be free. God is giving you the opportunity to be free. God put you here today to set you free. He chose you to be here. God is saying yes to you. He is waiting for you. He is waiting for you to say yes to Him. It is just that little step you have to make, one little step, to say yes to Him. But from your heart, not from your lips, from the heart: 'Yes, God!' 'Yes, God!' 'Yes, God!' 'Yes, God!'

Take a nice deep breath and let that old negative stuff go from you. And the Power was with God! And the Word was with God! And the Word said: Let there be Light! And there was Light. Instantly, He created everything. He created everything in His image. The Body of God is Light. Not millions of lights, just One Light. And you are It, just by saying, 'Yes, God!' You are making an opening here, you make a little opening in your heart, so the Light will start to shine.

We cut ourselves consciously off from this life and we live our tiny lives, not realizing the beauty we have. You have so much beauty and you don't even realize it. You'd rather live in the fear. What is this fear? It is darkness, it is shadows. Because, you know, when you are walking away from the Light, your shadow is in the front of you and you are always aware of it. When you walk towards the Light, your shadow is at the back of you and you are only aware of the Light. You are the Light. Recognize it in yourself. It's not outside of you, it's within you. It's within every one of you. If we were to take this Light out of every one of you, there would just be one ball of Light with one awareness.

What would that awareness be? I am I. I am all there is. There is nothing else. When you hurt one another, you hurt me, you hurt yourself, and everything comes back home to roost. Maybe not in this lifetime, but what you put out will come back. Give Light, you become Light. Play with the shadows, you only become the shadow. Truly I tell you: Love sets you free, but Love without conditions. You can never be free when you put conditions on your Love. You will become prisoner of the shadows, prisoner of the mind. And the shame is that most of you don't realize it!

So what is enlightenment? Is this only for the few? Of course not. Enlightenment: you *lighten up*. There are many films of me when I dematerialize. I just turn into Light. There are just one or two things I want to explain to you. In the Bible it says that if you speak with the Truth of God, you speak with the flaming sword, or you speak with the Light of God. In yoga, the highest point of speaking is with the 'I am'. This is when Vishnu, which is the Sky or the Mind, Brahma, which is the Word, and Iswara, which is the Heart, are connected. Vishnu, which is the Wisdom, Brahma, which is Love, and Iswara, which is the Action or the Power. When these three are in complete balance, the body becomes a matrix of incredible Power. The body becomes a pure crystal. When the Light coming through emanates from every direction, even in every orifice, the Light will come. So, when Brahma is speaking, Brahma is the Truth. The Truth is the Light, so you speak with the Light of God. This was the true meaning of Jesus' 'The Truth will set you free!' 'You will speak with the Light of God.'

I was giving a talk on Love in Spain, and as I was talking, the Light was coming out of my mouth, and they filmed it. Ninety per cent of the miracles that happened around me were always witnessed. I don't just say it. So, you see what then happens? When there is Wisdom, Love and Power, the triangle is upward, the triangle is here [points to forehead], this is the doorway. So, it is represented by an eye. The all-seeing eye is ever upon you. In other words, you become aware of your omnipresence in all three time periods, of the past, present and future. They are all happening at once, and there is a fluidic awareness – because awareness is beyond consciousness – of all things and all time periods.

This is why I say to you: God is *beyond* Love. You cannot comprehend God until you reach this stage. This is when you become God. Only God can understand God. Until you stop playing your games, you can never understand the Self. The mind has you. Have no doubt, it is very clever. To truly break away from its clutches, you have to stop thinking. And before we do any more, I am very conscious that some of you have to go to the toilet!

You know what is a shame today? You have not listened to one thing I said. You now, Divine Mother energized this room today. When you see the Divine Mother, she always comes with two angels. Divine Mother is very beautiful, I cannot even begin to tell you. But there are always two angels that accompany her. They are roughly the same size. They don't have wings. They are just in white, their hair is about as long as mine, very golden, and their complexion is a gold colour. But the Mother's complexion is like olive, so clear and beautiful, and when you come in the presence of her energy – wow! And you know, she came here today. She blessed you and she left her energy here. And what have you done with it? You go outside, make a noise, come back in here, making a noise, totally wiping out the vibrational force. And this is what I have been telling you about your monkey minds. I have been in prayer now with the Divine Mother to ask her to come and bless us again, to bring back that energy that her children have already forgotten.

What's the difference between you and a Master? A Master does not forget. The Master is always in the ever present, living only in the now, with a full presence of the Divine. Where are you? Where do you think you are? That's the place where you think you are. And if you look into your mind, you will see it's a dark place, a place of shadows, a place without sunlight, because the moment you put sunlight into it, like you did this morning, the shadows climb all over it to block it out. And you feel a victim of it. So, where is the Divine Mother now inside of you? It came out in words of the tongue. So, what should you practice? Practice silence. Within the silence, God speaks to you. Within the silence, the Divine Mother touches you.

You can't keep your body still because you can't keep your mind still. Remember what I said about giving your power over? You give your power to your mind and it will control you. It is the big boss and you are the slave. What you've done here today is only to show that point.

I keep telling you: only Love will set you free. Love. Why are you so afraid of it? One person came to me and said, 'Is that mind control?' Is Love mind control? When you can't even control your own mind, how can anyone control your mind? How do you catch your crazy monkey? You give it something to occupy itself with. And what do you give for the mind to be occupied? The Name of God. When you are thinking of God, no other thoughts can enter. The Name of God blocks everything out. It stops those unwanted thoughts. You know, when you are in love you cannot stop thinking about your lover. What she looks like, what's his name, what she smells like, what is he going to say to you – when you go out you are going to be together . . . You cannot stop thinking about your lover! Something is happening inside of you. The heart starts to become a flame. The passion starts to burn through your body. You cannot wait to come together with your lover. Just the mention of their name makes you feel, 'wow'! Have you experienced that? Put your hands up. Come on, you have never felt love? This is how it should be with the Name of God.

When you are thinking of the Name of God: passion, the feeling . . . Nobody can give you that feeling, it's something you have to experience. And yes, of course you will experience it if you have not already experienced it. And do you know what it is like when Divine Mother touches you? I am going to show you something. Who would like to see the Divine Mother? [Stephen approaches a woman in the audience]. Take your glasses off. First I will show you one of the Angels of Light. Tell me when you see the Light. Tell them what you are seeing.

MEMBER OF AUDIENCE: *White light.*

STEPHEN: Today the Divine Mother has blessed you! You think the Divine Mother is not real? She is more real than you are. You are not conscious of your own power in this life. The Divine Mother is conscious of all things. She is like the sea that overflows with Love. And if only you would say yes to her, perform the passion of your heart, you would see what I mean. Because there's no words in which I can express to you: the Love, the Power and the Wisdom.

Remember what I showed you. This is here [points to forehead]. Why is it there? Because it is the gateway between the higher and the lower self. And every chakra from here is down, because from here [the throat downward], this is the body. From the forehead upward it is the soul. When these eyes [points to physical eyes] are open, this eye [inner eye] is closed. When this eye [inner eye] is open, these [physical] eyes are closed. Unless they are not, of course. That means knowing how to keep all three eyes open. The three sacred points – three time periods.

All Power is now, all Wisdom is now, all Love is now. It's just in different degrees. You see, even though this eye is here in the middle, the eyes are the windows of the soul. Tell me, who lives in houses or flats? Maybe you live in a tent? So, do you have windows? Yes? Do you ever clean them? If the windows are not clean, they are dirty. This is the opposite of clean. And if the window gets really dirty, what do you do?

MEMBER OF AUDIENCE: *A cleaner comes.*

STEPHEN: This is the problem with most people, they are lazy. You see, the sunlight cannot come through a dark window, you only get fragments of light. You have to clean the window to get the full sunlight to come in, or clean the windows of the soul. The more you clean it, the more the light comes through. When you are in perfect harmony ... now because I am bringing the Light through my energy, it's vibrating much quicker. Heat will be coming from me now. Can you feel it here? You feel the heat?

Now I am creating a ball of light around my hand; just put your hand close to my hand. I created a miniature atomic bomb, if you like. You do this by the Light and your breath. I am giving you what the Masters do. I am giving you the secrets. You see, when you breathe, you are breathing in *prana*. But what is *prana*? How is it made? What is its function? How can you use it? Do you use it every day? How can you use it consciously, to improve yourself? These are all secrets laid down by the ancients, great Masters, years ago. And they practiced it. It's a science.

So, what is yoga? What does it mean? It means union. Union with what? With God? But you are God. With the Self. Why do you think the yogis do what they do? It's a science. It is a Divine Science. You see, you may live, say, 70, 80 years if you are lucky, at least in this body. And you have advanced 70, 80 years in this body. A Yogi is not happy with that. He wants to get there much quicker. Yogis don't advance 70, 80 years in one lifetime. They can advance one to two thousand years in one lifetime.

Go back to what Jesus said, 'Greater things than these shall ye do!' Who was He talking to, if He was not talking to you and me? Who was He talking to? He was talking to us. He found the way. And He says that all those who follow me, you can't come to the Father except through me. He was not using His ego; He found the way. He was talking about Christ Consciousness, which is inside all of us. And it works. He was saying, 'If you go this way, it will work for you!' But, human nature is lazy. If it cannot see immediate results, the mind will take you somewhere else. You may start with the mantra, you may go, 'Om, Om, Om... What am I going to do today? Om, Om, Om... What's for dinner? Om, Om, Om... What's on television? Om, Om, Om... Oh, I must do this! Om, Om, Om... Oh, I must do that! Om, Om, Om... Oh, I am tired! Om, Om, Om... I need to go to the toilet! Om, Om, Om... I need to eat something! Om, Om...'

You see, you play. You cannot play at this. It doesn't work. It will only send you crazy. When you are out of balance, the outcome affects the balance of the mind, so you will become unbalanced.

Many people want to be with the fairies. Okay, do it. But I have not yet found one who is balanced. Put your feet firmly on the ground, and put your mind in God. That which is above, is below. And that which is below, is above. There is only God. There is nothing else. And when you think of anything else, you are denying your own power. Love empowers you.

When you are in love, you can walk on the clouds. When you are in love, you can walk on water. When you are in love, you can turn that water into wine. It's that simple. And in some stage of your evolution, each one of you will be doing that. Maybe you find that hard to believe now, but in maybe thousands of years' time, evolution will take you to that point. It's not just the evolution of the body, it's also evolution of the consciousness. Life is about opportunities, to take them, to live them. But make sure the opportunities you are choosing are yours, not somebody else's. Give yourself totally to God and surrender, and it is no longer your will, but His that will be done.

Jesus said, 'Father, thy will be done!' He had such perfect faith! When he cured the sick or He raised the dead, it did not enter His mind that His Father will not do it. When people came into the Presence of this Passion, this Magnetism, they could not help but be touched. They couldn't help it. When you come into such a positive field of energy, so magnetized with love, how can the soul deny it? How can your soul deny it? Your soul wants to be free; don't you hear It crying out? Free me! Free me! Free me! Listen to It! Speak with It. Be free. God loves you! God loves you! God loves you! Free Yourself! Free Yourself now! Free Yourself now! Let it go! Say yes! Be freed by the Holy Ghost...

'You cannot come to the Father unless you come through me!' It means: you cannot come to God unless you live the Truth. That's what Jesus meant. He was the embodiment of Truth. He was the embodiment of Love. He showed it. He had such strength in Him that it set Him free. He was looking for the same freedom for you. He sees you as His own. He was the shepherd and we are His flock.

No shepherd lets one sheep go! You cannot be lost from Him. The moment you say *yes*, the moment you live the Truth, the Truth is inside of you. How much longer are you going to deny it? How much longer are you going to say no to it? Wake up! He came into this world to waken you. He died for you. He sacrificed Himself for you. Just to live the Truth.

What are you ready to sacrifice? You can't even sacrifice five minutes a day. And you call yourselves followers — of what? The only thing you follow is your stupid monkey mind. And you deny your strengths. I am here to tell you today: don't deny them anymore! Your strength is what makes you a human being. God never says no to you. Jesus never turned His back on you! Or you! Or you! Jesus never turned His back on anybody! They came to Him because He could see them. Jesus had eyes to see, He had ears to listen. Not like you. You have eyes, but you are blind. You have ears, but you are deaf. When was the last time you said, 'Thank you, God'? When was the last time you said, 'Thank you, God' from your heart? You are too busy with your mind. When did you look outside and say, 'Thank you, God, for such a beautiful day'? Did you get up this morning and say, 'Thank you, God'? I am here to wake! As you were eating your food, did you say, 'Thank you, God, for this food'? Did you wake up next to your partner, did you say, 'Thank you, God' for giving you such a beautiful person? When you were walking, did you say, 'Thank you, God, for my legs'? When you go to bed tonight, will you say, 'Thank you, God'? And when you are ready to go home, and the very last breath comes from your body, will you say 'Thank you, God, for the life you have given me'?

Jesus knew all this. He used the mantra of 'Thank you!' It is a mantra so powerful that He lived it. He lived the Truth. 'Thank you, God!' He thanked God all the time. Not one moment was He not in thanks, even when they put Him on the cross. He thanked. He fulfilled His destiny. He fulfilled His dharma. Why did He come to this world? You think it was easy for Him, knowing what was going to happen to Him? You think that must have been easy for Him?

You cry if you catch a cold! What if they would put wedges through your fists? You cry because your life doesn't go right for you. You cry all the time. 'God, why me!?' What strange people, eh?

Some say, 'Jesus was a sacrificial lamb.' He was far more than that. Far more… They say to me, 'Is Jesus back?' I say, 'Yes, He is back.' Look into the eyes of every child who is starving or dying, who is being abused; there you will see the Lord looking straight back at you! Now you tell me if you cannot see the Lord, you tell me if your eyes are blind and your ears are still deaf! You stand up and tell me now if you are still blind and still deaf! He is there. Next time when you go home and you have children at home, look in their eyes and you tell me you cannot see the Lord! Because the child has unconditional love for his mother, for his father. Is that what Jesus had? Did he not have unconditional Love – did He put conditions on anything? No, He loved for the sake of loving, for no other reason. His Love set Him free. Your love will set you free.

There is only one question: Do you want to be free? That's the only question – you answer yourself. Can you take your life now in your own hands? Can you live it with a passion that God intended you to live it? As a whole person, not as a fragmented person. Not as a persona that is so in pain, that only says 'No!' Who doesn't know the meaning of 'Yes!' One time you knew what yes was! Many, many lifetimes ago. But God sends His teachers into the world to say to you, 'Wake up!' The message is always the same: 'Wake up, before it becomes too late! Before you destroy everything!'

Look at the beauty of your country! It is magnificent! Feel it, feel the power of God in nature itself. He speaks to you all the time and you don't even listen to Him. You close your ears and you become deaf again. There is only this little voice saying, 'You do as I tell you!' This is your mind. Move it as Jesus showed you. And you know, you think that I am talking about religion? Then you are totally wrong. Jesus was not a Christian, He was a Jew, but he studied many religions, Buddhism and Hinduism, but was beyond religion. I am talking about Love. There is only one religion, that's the religion of the heart. True religion is Love. Love does not live in denial. Everything about us, every cell of our body, every feeling in it, is based on one or other emotion. Where do you choose to be now? Where do you choose to be? From this moment, what are you going to do with the life you now have, with the time that is left?

What can you take to God with you? Well, you know you can't take this body. You can't take your noble fame. You can't take your worth; people will be fighting over that when you are gone. There is only one thing you can take to God and that's your Truth. The only thing you can take is your Truth. When you stand naked in front of God, and he says, 'My child, what have you done?', most of you will lie. You will do it unconsciously. You will say, 'Lord, I have done my best!' And you know your best is not the Truth. You know you haven't done your best. You've been lying to yourself all your life.

So, how is an untruth going to blend with the Truth? How is the darkness going to blend with the Light? It cannot. You will come back again for more of your experiences. Do you want to be free? Then the answer is very simple: be free. No, there are no hard complications to what I say to you. I could write thick books of mysticism, I could come here and blind you with science. Nothing of that would get you to God. But what will get you to God is your Love. That's all. Your Love will get you to God. Your passion will get you to God.

You really believe God is not a real force. You may say, 'Oh yes, I believe in God!' But you don't believe in yourself! Shame on you! You look outside of yourself and you use every excuse. But the answer is in you, the Light is in you, the Truth is in you – yet you feel so sorry for yourself. Even when you come into this world and when you leave it, the play still goes on.

When you come into this life, when you are born, you are crying, and everybody around you is so smiling, 'What a beautiful baby!' Slap, slap! 'Such a beautiful baby! Oh, doesn't it look like...' Who? I don't know... A little bundle of skin and fat, it's supposed to look like somebody?! And the baby is crying and everybody is so happy.

It's coming to this world. But when you leave it you are smiling, and everybody around you is crying, 'I've lost my loved one!' Tell me: how do you lose Love? How? [A baby in the audience says, 'How?'] Isn't it beautiful? Isn't it so beautiful? Now, how can you live in denial, when you listen to such a thing?

Jesus had such a Love ... this is why, when you see a statue of Jesus, He is always blessing children, 'Come on to me, little children!' Can you, just for a moment, be still? Close your eyes. Reach out that Power of Jesus! It's such a Loving Power! It's so Compassionate! It's so strong! Wow, the whole room is filling with Light now! 'Yes, Lord! Enter my heart. Fill me with your Love. Strengthen me, Lord, that I may change that which can be changed and accept that which cannot be changed! Strengthen my understanding, Lord, so that I may be free; free to help, free to Love!' Wow, I will have to sit down!

Maybe if you open your eyes, some of you will see the Light coming from me. [After a while, a woman screams very loudly!] You think that power is outside of you? That power is within you, I reflected it back to you to let you know that those of you that have ears today will hear, those of you that have eyes today will see. Do not fear. You have the power to set yourself free, don't be afraid of it. I offer it to you as Jesus offered it. Come into the Light. But to live it every day of your life, to say 'Yes God', to get up, to say Yes to Him ... To use this wonderful mantra of 'Thank you' – you cannot believe how strong it is. Don't take my word, try it. From this moment, whatever you do, say 'Thank you, God!' Even for the sickness of your body, say 'Thank you, God!' He Loves you.

Jesus was a reflection of that Love. He stood in front of you, He put His hands out to you, and you have ignored them. Again He puts His hands out in front of you. Are you going to ignore Him this time? Are you going to turn your back? Are you going to deny Him again in this lifetime? How much longer can you deny the Truth? How much longer can you hide from this Light? You are using up your excuses. How many more are you going to make? How much longer are you going to wait?

Can you not hear God speaking to you? What is he saying? Come up higher! Come up higher! Come up higher! All the time he is telling us to come up higher! Stop playing with the filth and the dirt! Come into the Light! For two thousand years He has been saying the same message and every teacher that God has sent into the world has given the same message: Love – Love – Love. But what have you done with the messengers of God? First of all you put them on a platform, then you talk about them, then you beat them, then maybe you crucify them; then you praise them, then you make them into a saint . . . and all that time, you have lost the message. You have to wait another two thousand years.

How much longer are you going to wait for God? Or, how much is God going to wait for you? You see, there is a meeting point. There is a meeting point where both of you meet. I can tell you from my experience: that meeting point exists. It happened to me last year. And I could tell you such beautiful things. So beautiful . . . I don't have to read books. I have had my experiences with God. I have had my Love with Him. What more do I need? I am full of *Prema.*[*] I am full of *Ananda.*[†] What more do I need? Who can give me more? Only myself. I am in Love. What greater power is there than that? I am in Bliss. 'And the Angels of God told them there was a man.' Listen, listen to the bells of the angels. They are tolling for you. God is saying, 'Come up higher! I have sent my Beloved Son to you!' Do not deny the Truth any longer. I've come to answer your prayers. I've come to set you free. All those who have followed the Truth, you can't but know how to be free. Amen to that!

Don't be in fear. Don't let it get in your way. And the intellect too. Use your intuition. Truth always recognizes Truth. It is strange how few people recognize it. All Masters have a group of people that recognize the Truth within them. They are called disciples. Through thick and thin they will stay with the Master. They never lost the

---

[*] Love.
[†] Bliss.

path. Don't lose the path. You may not get another opportunity in this lifetime.

Sometimes there are no words, just as sometimes there is no Light. But you see, there is always Light, you are just not aware of it. When people are in this deep depression, it is so difficult to see the Light and be positive. Because we have lack of courage, lack the strengths in ourselves, or we think we do. But of course, it is not true. You know, we can empower or disempower ourselves. It is very simple to do it. People say, 'I want to be happy!' Why do you want to be happy? Why do you want to chase something that is always changing from day to day? Today you can be really happy. You get one phone call and your happiness is changed. So, why do we chase this thing called happiness? Why is it so important to us? Because it reflects our state of mind. It reflects how we think.

Our thinking is always in this state of flux. You are always changing your mind. What you put on today you will not put on tomorrow. What you think you do tonight, you may not do. You are always going to do big things in your mind, when later you don't think you have the strength to do them. What kind of strength am I talking to you about? Maybe the strength that Jesus had? Maybe there were saints stronger than Jesus? What about His mother who had to suffer, who had to watch her son go through this terrible torture. But she knew that her son could finish it. He had the power to say, 'I am stopping this game'. To walk away from it – but He didn't. And his mother knew that. So, she watched the play taking place, happening right in front of her. That strength, that is determination to see the game finished to the end. But we can't, because you are always changing your mind!

But you see, a Master does not change his mind. They are focused and they will stay focused until their reality changes. You always can change your reality just like that, you can change your thinking just like that, when you say *yes* to God or *no* to God. You don't need fancy words. You don't have to be in meditation one hundred hours a day. You need to live your meditation. Live it. What is the true meditation? Whenever you put yourself in touch with God, that is a state of meditation. So, how can you always be in a permanent state of meditation? Put yourself in a permanent state of God Awareness. You see, when you have realization, you realize there is no realization. There just is. All is God. Not one part of me is not His, just in different frequencies.

There is no special place to go. You go to your churches, because some of them perform miracles. You think there is power coming from the Church. This is not true. These are empty places until *you* go there. When you go there, you enter a part of your magnetism, and it's the magnetism that grows, attracting a like magnetism to you. So the place becomes full of energy, full of magnetism. You make it holy. And you make the days that you go there holy. But all places are holy. All days are holy. All minutes are holy. Everything is holy. You don't have to put yourself in one place to recognize it.

You know, Jesus said: 'Lift the stone, I am there! Split the wood, I am there!' This body is the Church! This body is the Synagogue! This body is the Temple! Where do you need to go? If you want to go to the temple, go within this Temple. Seek the Lord in this Temple – in your body. You think God is separate from your body? Impossible. Even the Bible tells you you're made in the image of God. We presume this image is Light.

What is science telling us? They tell us we are made of matter: atoms, protons, photons, electrons, life-trons ... and these are building blocks of life. So they are telling us how these are made: from condensed energy. Energy is condensed to matter. How is energy created? Light is condensed into energy. So, light is condensed into energy, energy is condensed into matter. This is the whole system of yoga. I am not the body and the body is not me.

MEMBER OF THE AUDIENCE: *We are who we are.*

STEPHEN: Even that is wrong. There is no we and I. There is no magic about this hidden strength. It's a world that is always filled with the water of life. You just have to know how to suck into it. And that is quite simple. First, recognize it. You can take nothing if you don't realize it exists. First realize it's within you, then you can take from it. Jesus did it, all the Masters do it. It's not special to any one Master. For a Master, the Truth is the Truth. It's the same Truth. It's the same Truth that lies within you. It's the same Truth that will set you free, because it puts you in command of your own energies. In other words, you take command of your life. No longer do you go backwards and forwards like a boat with no captain. When you take command, the boat will steer towards the land. There, you have freedom to be who you want to be. That is yourself.

No man can understand what love of a child for a woman is like. A man feels love for his children, of course. But the mother has a very special sensitivity. As a matter of fact, you women don't realize how lucky you are to be a woman. You know, it's a real honour to be a woman. Don't abuse that privilege, something God has given you. You know what I mean? Inside of you knows. But you know, we need to play parts in life. Man plays his part and the woman plays hers. And we step out together. We can step out together, but we must not step on each other. We must not take our partner's power away from them. They have every right to express their Truth and you have to express yours. But you know, when there is a meeting of minds and there is a meeting of the divine energy, the energy blends and grows ... and it can grow so big with so much power, with so much love, that it will knock you out.

I go to bed at night, I close my eyes, I just see Light. I look at you, I do not see bodies, I see a sea of Light. I am not worrying about what you think of me. I love you. That is the end of the story for me. But, do you love yourself? Are you ready to take control of your life? Are you ready to say *yes* to yourself now? You know, I know how it is in your lives. We've all been there; we all want different things. We want a good life, we want a good home, we want a good relationship, we want good children, we want good jobs, we want good food, we want lovely sunshine ... We want everything. We want! So, God says, 'Okay, keep wanting'. Instead of wanting, be positive. Instead of focusing on what you want, concentrate on what you are already, focus it with intention. Say *yes* to yourself. Is it easy? Some will find it easy, some will find it hard, but one thing everybody has to do – even Masters – they have to practice. That's what we have to do. Affirm what you already are, it will naturally attract to us. Use the law of attraction and magnetism.

A Master does not wake up in the morning and say, 'O, I am a Master!' A saint doesn't wake up and say, 'O, I think I will be a saint today!' Generally, you have to die to be a saint, like burned or crucified or something like that, or give some money to somebody. The Pope is very lovely – I think he has made one hundred saints in his lifetime. Wonderful. But, you see, we all have a potential saint inside of us, the same as we have a potential devil inside of us. It is a matter of choices. That's all it is, a matter of a choice. And if you have made a wrong choice today – remember what we said about the piece of paper? – tomorrow will come and then it is today. And when it is today, the page is empty. Make another choice. Make the choice that best suits you, then you are on the way to mastery. Making the right choices, or making the same choices if it is a good choice, because that choice best serves you.

How do you feel with that choice? Does it put a smile on your face? Does it make you say, 'Yes, God!' Or does that choice make you feel miserable? It's a matter of choices. But some people, you know, they are masochists, they enjoy punishing themselves. They want to punish themselves. They don't feel worthy of making the right choice. They live in the past and they try to run away from it. But where can you run? There is nowhere to go. If you look in the mirror here, you will see yourself. If you go to another country, you look in the mirror, you will see yourself. Where can you go? Where? There is nowhere. Nowhere to go, nowhere to hide. Your thoughts will follow you everywhere. You cannot hide from yourself, because you cannot hide from God. You see, God is the unseen witness to your actions. You cannot hide from Him. You really cannot hide from your own thoughts. They follow you through from heaven to hell.

Oh, you don't have to die to go to heaven and you don't have to die to go to hell. It's here and now. How you want it. There are many people that live in their own heaven and there are many people that live in their own hell, but they are only states of mind. That is simple to say, though that state of mind is very real to the thinker. Most of you have been there. As a matter of fact, there are only one or two places to be: in heaven or in hell — in love or in fear. There is nowhere else to be. It's your choice; nobody is making a choice for you, you are making it. So, don't blame somebody else. It's so simple to do that, to blame somebody else for us.

Why was I meditating when you were singing? I was centring with the roots of Light. I was going to ask something of them — if Jesus would transfigure me — but I don't know if this will work. But what we need to do really — the energy is gone down a little bit now — the reason for that is that you have eaten, you've made yourself tired, some of you are falling asleep . . . The energy is not as it should be. So I think we just need to lift this energy again, and I think to lift up this energy again we should ask our most beautiful sister if she could sing *Amen* and *Amazing Grace*. And if we can get the energy, I am sure the Lords of Light will try to manifest something. Now, it may happen when we are singing, it may happen after, it may not happen at all. I really can't make it happen. The last time this happened was in front of a Catholic bishop and several of his people. The transfiguration of Jesus was very wonderful. Now, what's the best way to see this? We need the lights out, and the best way is to close your eyes and to slowly open them, as if you are squinting, then to look at me, then look beyond me. Sometimes you will see something like a mist and in that mist there will be an impression of a face coming out and you might see my features or hands change. I really don't know. All we can do is try. We need to get this energy going.

The Power of the Lord is with us. The Power of the Lord is here with us. Jesus wants you to know that He loves you. Jesus is standing just here now. He says, 'All those that have eyes, see!' He is standing here. His Light is tremendous. It makes me feel quite dizzy. I can feel His hands on me. He touches me. My hands are not my hands. It is His hands. My lips are not my lips, they are His lips. His will is my will. He comes to give you Peace and Love, but you have to earn it. You have to work for it.

There are some other people He has brought. They are disciples. There is one here, Peter, and there is Paul, and Thomas. He says, 'I know what you are thinking, it is not true.' Now these three beautiful souls are passing through me. If you just stare, you will see the fleeting features of them. If you see them say, 'Yes!'

AUDIENCE: *Yes! Yes! Yes!*

STEPHEN: Let them know you see them, let them know that.

AUDIENCE: *Yes! Yes! Yes...!*

STEPHEN: Your voice tells them. If you see, say, 'Yes!'

AUDIENCE: *Yes! Yes! Yes...!*

STEPHEN: Now He is changing my face.

AUDIENCE: *Yes! Yes! Yes...!*

STEPHEN: Look at the hands. 'Speak to me ... speak to me ... speak to me...' The more you speak, the more He will show Himself. Watch me, God. 'I am the Light of the world.'

It was a little bit strange what we tried to do here today, because the lights should have been off. We should just use this light [points to small red light]. But He appeared anyway. He came. Maybe some of you saw Him, maybe some of you did not. But He came. And He brought two others with Him, more than two others. His Love and Power are so tremendous! It's very difficult to incorporate it in my body. I can try to show you the Light when Jesus comes. Did anybody manage to see it? Some of you did? Some of you did manage to see it. It is good. If the light was completely out, you would see it very clearly. But, you can't make it happen, you see. It is a question if it happens, it happens. But, anyway, He was with us and that is the main thing.

But Love is always with us, always with us. Love is a part of us.

Love is what we are. You don't have to go anywhere for it, you don't have to put yourself down, think bad things of yourself. Love is your very nature. Love is who you are. How can you keep denying it? How can you cocoon yourself off and live this little life without the true understanding of Love? You say you want to be free, but what is freedom without Love? What is freedom without expression – to express that Love from the heart of your being? It doesn't belong only to the Masters, it belongs to all of us. All of us have a share in it. All of us have the share. If you cut yourself off from the Light, you just become another shadow.

Take the Light, take it into you, blend with it; Light blends with Light. Love recognizes Love. That is the law of attraction. That's how God made things. His Law is perfect. Let this seminar end with one thing: a promise to yourself, a promise as from today, to change that which you don't like to that which you do like, that you can respect and you can love. As Baba would say to us: 'Start the day with Love, spend the day with Love, fill the day with Love, end the day with Love – this is the way to God.' No other way. Start to put it into practice as from now. First be kind to yourself, be kind to your loved ones, be kind to your family, be kind to your friends, be kind to strangers, be kind to animals – everything has something of God. The bird that flies free in the sky is God, the fish that swims in the sea is God, the ant that crawls on the ground is God. Even the flea that jumps on you is God. Everything has something of God.

And maybe if we will have another seminar, we will be able to turn all the lights out and this will work much better. But, He was here! So, I am going to wish you well. I know, without a shadow of doubt, God loves you. But can you love yourself?

MEMBER OF AUDIENCE: *Of course we do!*

STEPHEN: Of course you do. One day you will have to prove it to yourself. You know, I can still sense the essence of Jesus here. It's so beautiful!

Books to challenge **C** *your perception of reality*

A message from Clairview

We are an independent publishing company with a focus on cutting-edge, non-fiction books. Our innovative list covers current affairs and politics, health, the arts, history, science and spirituality. But regardless of subject, our books have a common link: they all question conventional thinking, dogmas and received wisdom.

Despite being a small company, our list features some big names, such as Booker Prize winner Ben Okri, literary giant Gore Vidal, world leader Mikhail Gorbachev, modern artist Joseph Beuys and natural childbirth pioneer Michel Odent.

So, check out our full catalogue online at
www.clairviewbooks.com
and join our emailing list for news on new titles.

office@clairviewbooks.com

CLAIRVIEW